PADRE PIO

PADRE PIO

Glimpse into the Miraculous

Pascal Cataneo

BOOKS & MEDIA

Boston

Library of Congress Cataloging-in-Publication Data

Cataneo, Pascal.
  [Padre Pio gleanings]
  Padre Pio, glimpse into the miraculous / Pascal Cataneo ; translated by Maureen McCollum and Gabriel Dextraze.
      p. cm.
  Translation of: Fioretti di Padre Pio
  Previously published under title: Padre Pio gleanings : Sherbrooke, QC : Editions Paulines, c1991.
  ISBN-13: 978-0-8198-5988-4
  ISBN-10: 0-8198-5988-5
  1. Pio, of Pietrelcina, Saint, 1887-1968. 2. Capuchins--Italy--Biography. 3. Stigmatics--Italy--Biography. 4. Christian saints--Italy--Biography. I. Title. II. Title: Fioretti di Padre Pio.
  BX4700.P7755C3813 2013
  282.092--dc23
  [B]

                              2012030678

The Scripture quotations contained herein are from the *New Revised Standard Version Bible: Catholic Edition,* copyright © 1989, 1993, Division of Christian Education of the National Council of the Churches of Christ in the United States of America. Used by permission. All rights reserved.

Cover design by Rosana Usselmann

Cover background photo: istockphoto.com/© Les Cunliffe

"P" and PAULINE are registered trademarks of the Daughters of St. Paul.

Translated by Maureen McCollum and Gabriel Dextraze

Originally published in Italian as *I Fioretti di Padre Pio* by Edizioni Dehoniane, Rome, 1988.

Copyright © 2013, Daughters of St. Paul

Published by Pauline Books & Media, 50 Saint Pauls Avenue, Boston, MA 02130-3491

Printed in the U.S.A.

www.pauline.org

Pauline Books & Media is the publishing house of the Daughters of St. Paul, an international congregation of women religious serving the Church with the communications media.

2 3 4 5 6 7 8 9   19 18 17 16 15 14

Contents

Introduction

I am privileged to have known Padre Pio personally. My first meeting with him took place at midday on June 17, 1940. I had just arrived from Bologna, Italy, where, the day before, I had been ordained a priest. I reached San Giovanni Rotondo, which was then quite different from the city it has since become. Before going to my own native village on Mount Gargano, I visited Padre Pio to consult him on a few personal problems, find out what he felt, and get his advice. I wanted to make a good start as a priest right from the very beginning.

Padre Pio received me in his cell, telling me he had not been able to go down to the chapel that day because of a severe headache. He immediately kissed my hands, as I was a new priest, and made himself completely available to me for as long as I wanted. At the end, he told me what he felt and gave me his advice.

To be honest, on walking out of his cell, I had the impression he had not given me more than any other priest I might have consulted. At that time I was also under the illusion that he had a kind of miraculous solution for every problem presented to him. In time I learned that Padre Pio intervened in a special way only when God moved him in that direction.

As a matter of fact, in all the years I knew and met with him, from 1940 until his death in 1968, I experienced extraordinary interventions on very few, rare occasions. It is mostly through other people, intimately connected with him, and through the numerous biographies written about him, that I have put together what is recorded here.

In this way I have become aware of the many sides of his personality harmoniously blended into a deep humanity and profound spirituality, which spontaneously manifested itself in many circumstances. I want to show this through this variety of episodes, which I call *I Fioretti di Padre Pio* [the Little Flowers of Padre Pio], not because they have entered into the realm of legend, but because they have an aura of mystery surrounding them.

Twenty years after his death, the picture of Padre Pio, far from fading, has taken on the dimensions and bearing of a giant in faith. One day, when a Brother remarked that the large number of visitors attracted by Padre Pio meant a great deal of extra work for those around him, Padre Pio replied prophetically, "This is nothing to what it will be one day!" On another occasion he said, "Wait a while . . . and you will see how truth will fly at you."

We now see the fulfillment of those words. My desire is to contribute in some small way to a better understanding of Padre Pio by offering these "gleanings" for our reflection. I believe that what is written here, presented in a style acceptable to our contemporaries, will help build up that Kingdom of God so much needed by our world.

PASCAL CATANEO

CHAPTER 1

A Powerful Vision

To understand better what motivated Padre Pio through-out his life, we must keep in mind a very special vision he had in 1902. He later spoke of this significant event to his confessor, in the third-person singular, using his baptismal name, Francis.

A man of majestic appearance and rare beauty, shining like the sun, stood beside Francis and took him by the hand. After reassuring him he gave Francis this invitation: "Come with me for you must fight like a valiant warrior." Francis was led to a vast countryside, through a multitude of men divided into two groups. On one side were very handsome men dressed in robes that were as white as snow. On the other side were very ugly men dressed in black robes and who appeared to be more like dark shadows.

The young man, standing between these two groups, saw a giant creature coming toward him. His forehead touched the clouds and he had horrible features.

The mysterious person in the shining white robes stand-ing at his side told Francis to fight the monster. Francis begged to be spared from the fury of this strange being but was told:

"You cannot escape this. You must fight. Courage! Go, fight boldly and with confidence. I will be here beside you to help you, and I will not allow the creature to defeat you."

The battle began and it was terrible. Helped by the resplendent person in white, Francis had the upper hand. The monster was forced to retreat, followed by all the ugly, shadowy men, shouting, screaming, and cursing at the top of their voices. The handsome group in white robes applauded and praised the one who had helped Francis in this hard battle.

The resplendent one, who shone brighter than the sun, placed an indescribably beautiful crown on Francis' head but removed it immediately saying: "Another crown, more beautiful than this, will be yours if you learn to fight this creature you have just defeated. He will always be back to attack you. Fight bravely and count on my help. Don't be afraid of being harassed by him nor terrified by his horrible appearance. I will be with you, and I will help you every time so that you will be victorious over him."

Padre Pio was called, in an extraordinary way, to wage war against the forces of evil, against those who assail mankind, against those who direct these forces and represent them, to help build up the Kingdom of God.

This struggle would be enacted, directly or indirectly, a thousand and one times, in various ways. The events reported in these pages offer only a few examples. They are, however, numerous enough to amaze us. May they also inspire us to advance on the path of spiritual maturity, to the point of finding perfection in the fullness of Christ!

CHAPTER 2

A September Morning, 1918

Padre Pio received the stigmata, or wounds of Christ, on September 20, 1918. This event determined his destiny and made him a powerful sign to the world.

What does this phenomenon mean? It probably parallels what St. Paul said of himself when he wrote, "I am now rejoicing in my suffering . . . in my flesh I am completing what is lacking in Christ's afflictions" (Col 1:24).

What is lacking in Christ's suffering? Absolutely nothing! His sufferings have an infinite value and redeem the whole world without any extra help from us. If something is lacking, it is because God decides it is lacking, and this is humanity's free participation in its own redemption. Here we have to understand the Christian meaning of sin as the rejection of God's love. In sin, we have what St. Augustine calls "a love of creatures to the point of contempt for God." This is a love that goes beyond the law of God and brings a pleasure that separates us from God. God is loved by detaching oneself from the inordinate love of creatures. This detachment is as painful as setting a dislocated bone, only here we are speaking of love. It is not a matter of accepting suffering for the sake of suffering. This is neither human nor even Christian, but suffering is an essential component of love.

Padre Pio's stigmata caused him continual and intense suffering. The Lord asked from him an extraordinary participation to "completing what is lacking in Christ's afflictions" (Col 1:24). He accepted with all his heart whatever God asked of him. Sometimes, when asked by his spiritual sons about the suffering the stigmata caused him, he lifted the veil a little to reveal a sight terrifying to anyone.

He particularly spoke of what he endured while celebrating Mass, during which, in some degree, he lived again the passion of Christ. When others, however, offered to share his terrible agony, Padre Pio would tell them he was jealous of his sufferings and that he would not give them up to anyone! This showed his great love of God and for souls. He not only accepted his suffering but desired it to save the numberless sinners who crowded around him.

The event

No one actually saw Padre Pio receive the stigmata. On that day, his Superior, Father Paolino da Casacalenda, was at San Marco in Lamis, a village near San Giovanni Rotondo. The other members of the community were out. Everything took place between Padre Pio and the Lord, in deepest intimacy, before the crucifix that can still be seen in the tribune above the entrance to the little church.

Padre Pio did not want this occurrence to become known, but the time came when his Provincial Superior, Father Benedetto, from San Marco in Lamis, insisted that Padre Pio write an account of the incident. On October 22, 1918, Padre Pio agreed and wrote the following:

> On the 20th of last month, in the tribune after the celebration of Mass, I was overcome by a state of repose like a deep and peaceful sleep. All my senses, interior and exterior, as well as the faculties of my soul, were plunged into an indescribable stillness. In addition, there was a total silence within me and around me followed by a deep peace. Then, in a flash, I saw before me someone like the mysterious person I had seen on August 5, but with one difference: His hands, feet, and side were running with blood . . .

Padre Pio was in great distress and deeply distraught. Engulfed in pain he could not rise from the floor and had to crawl, on all fours, back to his cell, leaving a trail of blood in the corridor. He tried to wipe away the blood as best he could and then hid the wounds with bandages.

On returning to the monastery, Father Paolino, the Superior, noticed that Padre Pio was behaving rather strangely, but he did not give this a second thought. Gradually, he began to sense that Padre Pio was hiding something from him. He questioned him, but Padre Pio gave nothing away. Somehow, Father Paolino heard talk of the stigmata. He was suspicious and wanted to get to the bottom of things. One day he walked into Padre Pio's cell without knocking on the door and discovered the secret. He immediately informed the Provincial Superior who urged the greatest prudence in the matter and asked Padre Pio to write down all that had happened to him.

From that moment a strongly emotional atmosphere surrounded the Padre Pio, ranging from cult-like devotion to violent aversion! This would be his Calvary. Until the day he died, Padre Pio would be a sign of contradiction.

"Hey! What are you doing?"

At first, Padre Pio took great care to hide his wounds, not only from visitors but also from his brothers in religion. One of them, who was quite close to him, noticed that the priest was so completely taken up with the sufferings he bore for the love of Christ and the salvation of souls, that he had not changed his socks for a long time. One day, when Padre Pio was ill, this young Brother, who was looking after him, suggested that it might be good for Padre Pio to have his feet washed. Padre Pio let him do it. His confrere was able to see that Padre Pio's feet were covered with scabs that made it difficult for him to walk. The Brother scraped off the scabs with great care, washed and dried Padre Pio's feet, and then kissed them before putting Padre's sandals back on. At this, Padre Pio called out, "Hey! What are you doing?" The Brother explained that this was the custom whenever he washed anyone's feet. "Well," said Padre Pio, "you can do that to other people but not to me!"

Capuchin versus Benedictine

Padre Pio had been suffering for a long time from a severe hernia that caused him pain and difficulty when walking. He had always avoided having an operation—until the day he could no longer stand the pain and consulted a surgeon. The doctor, Giorgio Festa, was one of his converts and very devoted to Padre Pio. A room in the monastery was prepared for the operation on October 10, 1925. When the moment came for the patient to be put under anesthesia, Padre Pio refused it and said, "Will you be able to resist looking at my wounds?"

The doctor replied, "No!" with great frankness. "Now you see why I cannot allow myself to be put to sleep!" said Padre Pio.

The surgeon pointed out that the operation would be long and painful, but Padre Pio had been ordered by his Provincial to hide his stigmata, and he wanted to obey even at the price of such suffering. He refused the anesthesia. Dr. Festa asked him to drink at least a little Benedictine liquor to sustain him. He took some. When the doctor offered a second glass, Padre Pio cut him short, saying, "No! That's quite enough; otherwise there will may be a fistfight between the Capuchin and the Benedictine!"

The operation was performed and, as expected, was very painful. Padre Pio endured the suffering with superhuman strength. In the end, he fainted as he was being taken to his cell. Dr. Festa took advantage of this situation to hurriedly examine the stigmata in the presence of two of the Brothers and so got what he wanted in spite of Padre Pio's protests.

CHAPTER 3

From Far and Wide

People flocked to Padre Pio. Generally, they were men and women who wanted to leave behind a life of sin. He led them to God. His methods of conversion were matter for discussion. Padre Pio could be quite blunt and even, at times, violent; this was rather misleading. There were profound reasons for this behavior. It was pointed out to him that his harshness was disconcerting and could distance souls from him. He replied, "I treat souls as God wants me to treat them." And there were those God indicated to him who needed to be shaken up, otherwise they would not give up their evil ways.

We know that some illnesses can be treated with medicine while others need surgery. We generally turn to surgery when medication fails. I think Padre Pio could be considered a "surgeon of souls." When he was hard on someone, that man or woman might well be annoyed and even resentful, but if the desire for conversion was genuine, he or she would come back to Padre Pio. This way of acting was not a vent for Padre Pio's anger but a tactic for saving souls.

About six weeks after Padre Pio's death, I went to pray at his grave. At that time I wanted to meet with Father Pellegrino Funicelli who had assisted him in his last moments. I asked him about Padre Pio's brusqueness, and he told me he had personally witnessed one of these outbursts. It concerned a woman at the monastery door. As soon as the door was closed and Padre Pio had gone inside, he became calm and serene, as if nothing had happened. Father Funicelli pointed out to me that normal anger generally does not die down so quickly.

There were other reasons for this harsh behavior. Padre Pio, who was more clearly aware than anyone of his position as a creature of God, could not stand the veneration and fanatical outpourings directed at him by so many people, and so he was driven at times to react strongly against such behavior. It has to be said, however, that beneath his rough exterior lay a very tender and sensitive heart. Padre Pio was probably trying to protect himself from the weakness of his own human nature. This type of conduct on his part has to be prudently considered for what it is worth.

Beniamino Gigli in trouble

In a popular magazine, the mother of the famous Italian tenor Beniamino Gigli told the story of her son's first meeting with Padre Pio. The tenor wanted to meet the priest after he had heard various stories from friends about the extraordinary things Padre Pio did. The singer arrived at San Giovanni Rotondo in a luxurious car with a uniformed chauffeur and aroused a great deal of curiosity. At this time he had already established an international reputation.

When Gigli was introduced to Padre Pio, the priest gave him that searching look that went to the heart of things without being influenced by appearances. Padre Pio went up to Gigli and attacked him point blank: "You call yourself 'Gigli,' like the lily, which is a symbol of purity, but you are a sullied lily because you are cheating on your wife and have a secret relationship with another woman. You call yourself 'Beniamino,' which means beloved of God, but God does not love you at all because of the state of your soul."

One can imagine how upset the tenor was on hearing this. Padre Pio had read in Gigli's soul what others chose to ignore, and he had confronted him with his responsibility. Beniamino, however, had the strength and humility to accept the brutal indictment. He changed his ways, broke off his extramarital relationship, and, until his death, was a faithful friend of the priest. In his later years Gigli often visited Padre Pio for advice and comfort.

Padre Pio was always very happy to see Gigli and often asked him to sing his best known song, "Mamma," because it made him think back, with great tenderness, on his own mother, Peppa. More often than not, Padre Pio did not hear the song to the end because it moved him so much that he went away to cry.

"Go back to 1936!"

The comedian and actor Carlo Campanini, who is buried in the San Giovanni Rotondo cemetery, first met Padre Pio in 1939, but it took another eleven years before Campanini really changed his life for the better.

His first meeting with the priest was not motivated by anything religious but, quite simply, for material benefit. The actor was constantly on the road and away from his family who lived in Rome. He was rather unhappy about this and wanted work that would bring him closer to home. One day a colleague told him about a cousin who had sorted out some family problems, thanks to the good offices of Padre Pio. Carlo wanted a similar favor. At one point he was in Bari and took advantage of this to go on to San Giovanni accompanied by a friend who would introduce him to Padre Pio.

It was Holy Week, and the priest was more than ever lost in deep meditation on the passion of Christ. The two friends arrived late and got into the monastery only after a great deal of persistence! When he saw them, Padre Pio exclaimed, "Even during Holy Week they won't give me any peace! What do you want?" Campanini and his friend answered that they wanted to go to confession. Padre Pio said to them, "Go and make your preparation in the church. I will hear your confession after Mass tomorrow." They went away and returned next morning as agreed. Campanini was very moved by Padre Pio's Mass, despite thinking that it would never end because he was kneeling in a very awkward position. The Mass over, he went to confession and was taken aback to hear the priest cite his sins one by one. Before giving absolution, Padre Pio made Campanini promise to change his life. Campanini really wanted to speak about his actual reason for coming—to find work in Rome in order to be near his family—but he did not have the courage to do so. However, he made his request interiorly, from the depth of his heart, with much insistence.

Back in Rome, Campanini was unexpectedly called to Cinecittà studios to read for an important role in the film *Addio, giovinezza* (*Goodbye, Youth*). The candidates for the part included many actors much better known than Campanini, but he was the one chosen. This opened up for him a career that made him rich and famous. He had parts in over 100 other films in quick succession! By the end of 1949, he had reached the height of his success and wealth. But he had not kept the promise made to Padre Pio about changing his life, and this deeply troubled him.

One day Campanini's wife announced that she wanted to consecrate the family to the Sacred Heart. She had spoken of it to their pastor, and he had suggested that, for such an occasion, it would be good that she and her husband go to confession and Holy Communion. Campanini did not dare go against his wife's wishes and told her he would give it some thought. The consecration was fixed for January 8, 1950.

Two days before, on the feast of the Epiphany, Campanini was walking in Rome when he happened to pass by a church. He went in with the intention of going to confession, but when he saw the priest, who was a very large, overweight man, he changed his mind. Looking around he saw another priest, who was slightly built, praying before a crucifix. Soon the slim priest got up and went to the confessional to take over hearing confessions. The priest had hardly sat down when he called Campanini and offered to hear his confession. The comedian agreed and was quite radiant when he left the church. He realized that he could now return to Padre Pio without having to confess all the sins he had committed up until that time, and thus Padre Pio would be unaware that he had not kept his promise!

As arranged, the consecration of the Campanini family took place in their home. Later Campanini took advantage of an opportunity offered and went to visit Padre Pio, expecting that he could make an "ordinary" confession to him. The priest, however, who cared about the actor and had his protection at heart, wanted Campanini to wipe his soul clean and so said to him, "Begin from 1936!" Campanini tried in vain to convince Padre Pio that it had not been that long since his last confession, but Padre Pio was quite inflexible: "Begin from 1936!" Campanini did as he was told, and from that time on he and Padre Pio forged a strong spiritual bond and a deep friendship that lasted until the Campanini's death.

"Why are you here with us?"

One of the conversions brought about by Padre Pio resulted in a chain reaction. It was that of the lawyer Cesare Festa, an avowed and prominent Freemason, cousin of Padre Pio's personal doctor, Giorgio Festa. One day Giorgio challenged his cousin to visit Padre Pio and see for himself the supernatural powers he denounced so strongly. The lawyer accepted the challenge and went to San Giovanni Rotondo. Padre Pio was talking with some people when he noticed Cesare Festa. Immediately Padre Pio left the group and confronted the lawyer: "Well! Why are you here with us? You are a prominent Freemason." The lawyer agreed. Padre Pio then asked, "What is the duty of freemasonry?" The lawyer replied, "To overthrow the Church."

After this preamble, which no one had expected, Padre Pio changed his clothes, took the lawyer by the hand, and invited him to follow him. Padre Pio told the story of the Prodigal Son simply and effectively. Suddenly Cesare identified with the young man and, even more, began to feel very intensely the love that God has for those who stray from him. Cesare gave in and went to confession, and when he got up from his knees, he had the impression that he had been born again into a new kind of life.

Some days later he went back to Padre Pio who wrote these words for him on the title page of a New Testament: "Blessed are those who listen to the word of God, guard it jealously, and accomplish it faithfully." This was a warning and an exhortation to Cesare to be rooted in his new state of grace. The lawyer understood and welcomed this. He resolved to remain faithful to this new way of life.

One day he decided to go on a pilgrimage to Lourdes. When members of the Freemasons' Lodge in Genoa heard of this, they became alarmed at the possible consequences of such a conversion. They called a meeting to solemnly condemn this turncoat. In no way intimidated, Cesare Festa decided to attend the meeting. As he was leaving for the meeting, someone brought him a letter from Padre Pio encouraging him not to be ashamed of his faith and to fight: "The Lord will help you." At the meeting, the former Freemason explained his conversion and rigorously defended the Church. After this he became a fervent Christian and a devout follower of Padre Pio.

*"O! Man from Genoa, you are close to the sea,
but you do not know how to wash yourself!"*

Among the chain of conversions brought on by that of the lawyer Cesare Festa was that of Dr. Ezio Saltamerenda, Director of the Institute of Biotherapy in Genoa. A convinced atheist from youth, the doctor took every possible occasion to advance his ideas. On hearing of Dr. Festa's conversion, Dr.

Saltamerenda wanted to see this Padre Pio for himself, so he set out for San Giovanni Rotondo. Padre Pio had never seen this man before, but he noticed him in the crowd and addressed him personally: "O! Man from Genoa, you are close to the sea, but you do not know how to wash yourself!"

Saltamerenda was shaken to his roots by this soul-analysis. How was this priest able to identify him and depict his soul with such precision? Could it be that the supernatural, which he had so long denied, really did exist after all? He began to see that he had to wash his soul of its stains just as he washed his body. Overcome by revulsion with his spiritual state, which had been revealed to him so suddenly, he wanted to confess his sins to Padre Pio. The priest knew that Dr. Saltamerenda was not ready to confess and that his soul was not lucid enough to benefit from the grace of God. Padre Pio refused. Aware of his condition, Saltamerenda was very ill at ease. His soul was disturbed, his mind in a quandary, when, suddenly, a very strange thing happened: He noticed a strong scent of violets surrounding him. Brother Francis came across him in this state of extreme anxiety. When the doctor explained the reason for his crisis, Brother Francis took him by the hand to the cell of Padre Pio, whose tactics he knew very well! As soon as the door opened, Saltamerenda again detected the scent of violets wafting around him. This time, Padre Pio welcomed the doctor with kindness; and during Saltamerenda's confession the priest listed, one by one, all the sins the doctor had committed since childhood and then gave him absolution.

From that moment, Saltamerenda became a devoted follower of Padre Pio, and, with the same enthusiasm he had shown for spreading his atheistic ideas, he now set out to make Padre Pio known.

The perfumed poster

The internationally acclaimed sculptor Francesco Messina had been brought up without any religious instruction whatsoever and, as an adult, was far from being a practicing Catholic. A pragmatist by nature, he had no time for stories of miracles. In the spring of 1945, he organized an exhibition of his work in Genoa. This was advertised on posters throughout the city. One evening he and his wife went to dinner with friends who were very devoted to Padre Pio. They talked at length about the Capuchin of Gargano and showed the sculptor a thick biography of the priest. Messina leafed through it and was particularly struck by Padre Pio's penetrating eyes in one of the book's photographs.

After dinner Messina and his wife went back to their hotel, but he could not sleep because of the effect of those penetrating eyes. Around five o'clock in the morning he was aroused from his sleep by the telephone. Who could it be? What news could justify such an early call? Because it was so early, and he did not get much sleep, Messina was in a foul mood when he answered. His irritation grew when a childhood friend called to tell him that he had smelled the perfume of Padre Pio coming from a poster advertising his exhibition in Piazza de Ferrari. His friend went on to say that this "coincidence" could be explained. The perfume was calling Messina to go immediately to Padre Pio. This friend on the telephone was none other than Saltamerenda, and he insisted Messina go! Messina was about to tell him that he could "to go to hell," but he controlled himself. Instead, he told his insistent friend that he would think about it, and then he excused himself and said he had important work to do in Milan.

He did, in fact, leave for Milan, but the thought of Padre Pio would not leave him alone. Finally, he decided that he really had to meet this man. A short time later he contacted Saltamerenda, and together they went to San Giovanni Rotondo. It was late when they arrived at the monastery, and Padre Pio had already retired to his cell. Saltamerenda insisted on going in, and because the community knew him well, he got his way. Padre Pio was a bit cross with Saltamerenda and turned to Messina and said, "And what do you want?" Messina replied that for a long time he had wanted to meet him, and now that he had done so, he wanted to place himself in the priest's hands. Padre Pio replied rather abruptly, "You certainly are in good hands!" Padre Pio told them to go to the church and prepare for the sacrament of Confession, and he would come down later. Messina wanted to say that he did not feel psychologically or spiritually ready for confession, but the priest had already walked away. When Padre Pio came down to the church later, Messina hastened to tell him that he was not at all ready. Padre Pio stopped him in his tracks: "Listen, don't say anything and just answer me." He then began a detailed review of all Messina's sins from childhood until that moment. Messina paled and then surrendered, faced with this kind of spiritual projector that pitilessly unfolded before him all the tortuous ways of his soul. The next day he attended Padre Pio's Mass and went to Holy Communion.

His life changed radically. He became one of Padre Pio's most faithful spiritual sons. He used to say, "I was born on April 11, 1949." This was the day he had met Padre Pio. Until the priest's death, Messina visited the priest frequently and sculpted the monumental Way of the Cross that can be seen today on the way up the hill near the Church of Santa Maria delle Grazie at San Giovanni Rotondo.

"That is heresy!"

The case of Frederick Abresch is seen as a milestone in the list of conversions attributed to Padre Pio. This man, German by origin, had turned from Protestantism to Catholicism, not by conviction but for convenience. He went in for studies of the occult, which gave him no peace. Now and then he would come to church only under sufferance because his wife was a devout Catholic and a follower of Padre Pio.

Urged by his wife, Frederick Abresch went one day to San Giovanni Rotondo to meet this priest who did such extraordinary things. His first meeting took place in December 1928. He was initially quite indifferent—until he went to confession. Padre Pio told Abresch that in previous confessions he had held back grave sins, and Padre Pio asked him if he was really serious about confessing. Abresch tried to justify the matter by explaining that he considered confession a useful convention but could not accept that it was supernatural. Padre Pio's expression became extremely stern and sad, and he cried out, "That is heresy!" Then he told Abresch that all his communions had been sacrilegious and that he had to start again from zero! The man would have to prepare himself by going back to his last "good" confession. Padre Pio then went off to hear other confessions. Abresch was so devastated by Padre Pio's words that he could not recall his past.

When the priest returned to the sacristy, he found the poor man still in a state of utter bewilderment. Padre Pio then took the initiative and, by careful questioning, paraded Abresch's whole life before him and finished by saying, "You have been singing a hymn to Satan while Jesus, in his divine love, has been breaking his neck for you!"

After this crystal-clear reading of his soul, Abresch felt a deep sense of repentance. When he left the confessional pardoned, he felt rejuvenated and filled with unspeakable joy. Things did not stop there. His wife, who had first encouraged her husband to meet Padre Pio, found herself in a very painful situation. Doctors had advised an operation with side effects that would prevent her from having children. She ardently desired to be a mother. Abresch asked Padre Pio's advice. After having prayed, the priest said, "No operation!"

From that moment his wife felt completely cured. Two years later Padre Pio predicted that Abresch and his wife would have a son who would become a priest one day. This prediction was fulfilled.

Nair, the red pasionaria of Emilia

There was a woman in Bologna, who was one of those people who when they take up a cause give themselves completely to it. For her, it was all or nothing! Her name was Italia Betti, but she was known as Nair. Her cause was the struggle for human justice. She firmly believed from the outset that this battle could only be won by communism.

Born into a poor family of thirteen children, she had made enormous sacrifices to get her doctorate and become a teacher of mathematics and physics at the Galvani High School in Bologna. As a member of the Communist Party, she became a fervent militant. Her commitment had a kind of religious charism about it. After many years on this road, she became weary, physically and morally, because she began to realize that communism did not have the solutions to the cause she had given her life to—that of justice.

During this period Betti had a dream about Padre Pio. He stood beside a house that brought terror to anyone who went inside. The choice was offered: either go into the house in terror or remain outside in peace. She was impressed by this dream and wanted to solve the puzzle. She decided to speak with Padre Pio in person. Betti went to San Giovanni Rotondo with her mother and sister on December 14, 1949. They attended Padre Pio's Mass, and this celebration opened up such spiritual dimensions for her that she felt compelled to reflect on them. She spent a good two hours in the church. When, afterward, she went to Padre Pio for confession, she understood that the struggle for true justice can only be realized within the context of a Christian view of life. She became a convert and expended all her energies on the spiritual path indicated by the priest. Betti no longer wanted to leave San Giovanni, and so she left behind all that she had in Bologna and had a small house built near the man who had influenced her conversion. Betti died on October 26, 1950, and in her last will and testament she wrote:

> My return to the Church, after I had rejected it for twenty years, was done knowingly and not simply through fear of losing my life. It was the result of my conscience crying out for peace. It did not take long for me to come to the profound understanding that life was not what I had been living up to that time. I understood also, in an indisputable way, that it was absurd to think of humans—those little organized molecules of the universe—as the coordinators of all human sciences. Man is a divine creation, so he must feel part of it all and not be an end in himself. He must recognize that he is

only a little particle of energy that constantly needs a guide to help him go on.

"That's quite enough!"

Giovanni Bardazzi, a good Tuscan, was not lacking in ardor or daring. He had joined the ranks of the Communist Party in Prato and had been put in charge of a party branch. His one aim was to restore order according to communist ideology. He could not bear the sight of priests, monks, or nuns. One day he found some Sisters in his house. He threw them out and turned on his wife, who had let them in. He wanted all churches turned into dance halls, and he worked toward this goal like a madman.

One night, in a dream, he saw a bearded friar, his hands in mittens, who said to him, "That's quite enough! It's time to stop all this! I am waiting for you at San Giovanni Rotondo." Bardazzi was very disturbed by this dream. Who could this religious be? Where is San Giovanni Rotondo? He spoke to his wife who not only told him who the friar was and where he could find San Giovanni Rotondo, but also encouraged him to go there and clear up what was going on in his mind. He was hesitant: "Will I go, or won't I?" After some time he decided that he had to get to the bottom of it all, and so he set out for San Giovanni Rotondo with his wife and some friends.

On arriving, he sent his wife and friends off to the monastery while he sought the local Communist Party headquarters. He had no doubt they would fill him in on this hoaxer. To his utter amazement, his comrades were far from sharing his views on the priest. No one meddled with Padre Pio! Bardazzi could not understand and labeled them lukewarm communists. The only thing to do was to go to the monastery and check out this man himself. When he arrived, another surprise lay in store. A crowd waited to get into the church, praying as they waited, with rosaries in hand—even the men! He understood less and less. What kind of world was this?

He told himself he would talk to this priest next day and "put him straight." He was convinced that all this was a hoax to deceive poor people. But he would not be taken in by it! Padre Pio arrived, and Bardazzi went forward and started to tremble all over! What the devil was going on? On reaching him, Padre Pio said very quietly, "The black sheep has returned." "Good God! Some compliment!" thought Bardazzi. The poor man suddenly found himself engulfed in a strange atmosphere and heading for a very disturbing spiritual crisis.

The next day he went to Padre Pio's Mass, which was then celebrated in the old chapel. Bardazzi placed himself so that he could see every move of Padre Pio. When the friar turned around and extended his arms at the "Pray brethren . . . ," his hands were bare, and the stigmata, surrounded by blood, could be clearly seen. Everyone present was astounded and deadly silent because of the suffering they saw on the priest's face. Bardazzi wanted proof. "If it is true that this priest suffers the passion of Christ at this moment, why couldn't he, Bardazzi, have some share of it too?" What a thought! Suddenly, an intolerable pain seized him. It lasted only an instant, but it seemed like an eternity to Bardazzi.

This is how the fiery, hotheaded Tuscan was introduced to the supernatural ambience surrounding Padre Pio. He was perplexed by it. He saw things in a different light, the light of grace, and became aware of his own sinfulness. He wanted to go to confession, but Padre Pio asked him, "Tell me, what has the Lord done to you?"

Bardazzi replied, "Nothing! I don't even know if he really exists."

"What do you mean, you don't know if he really exists? Of course he exists!"

The two men entered into a serious dialogue that led nowhere. To Padre Pio this man was not ready, and he told him so in no uncertain terms: "I cannot give you absolution because I don't want to go to hell because of you!"

Bardazzi was plunged into the deepest darkness of his spirit. He racked his brains, questioned his conscience, and decided to get out of this mess, enlightened and convinced. Little by little, with the help of God's grace and Padre Pio's prayers, light began to flood the Tuscan's soul. He saw himself with the eyes of Christ and sincerely asked forgiveness. Then he went to Padre Pio who gave him absolution. A totally transformed Bardazzi returned to Prato. He left the Communist Party and endured the taunts of his former comrades. He showed the strength of soul and spiritual certitude that were his, with the help of Padre Pio, and began a new life.

A slow conversion

Conversion is not always an instant affair. Sometimes it comes in stages and adapts to the state of the soul that needs to move slowly to assimilate the truths of faith, one by one. Such a person was Alberto del Fante. He was a notorious Freemason from Bologna. In his bitterness, he had written a great deal of abuse against the Church. In the newspaper, *Italia laica*, he had described Padre Pio as a hoaxer, a charlatan, and a fraud, and accused him of taking advantage of people's naivety.

One of del Fante's nephews came down with an incurable illness. The doctors had given up all hope. One day, without del Fante knowing, a friend of his asked for the nephew's cure through the intercession of Padre Pio. The cure came quickly and was, humanly speaking, inexplicable.

When del Fante heard about the intercession of Padre Pio, he was utterly astonished and intensely curious. He decided to go to San Giovanni Rotondo to meet this man. His interviews with Padre Pio went on for days. The priest put himself completely at the disposal of the Freemason explaining everything he wanted to know about the faith. Del Fante was torn between two disturbing realities: the incontestable cure of his nephew against all human odds and the indisputable fact that, despite never having met or known Padre Pio, the priest knew all about del Fante's present life and his future! Gradually del Fante was moved toward conversion and kept a diary of his spiritual journey.

One by one, all his doubts faded to the point where his soul was completely enlightened. He not only became a convert but a follower of Padre Pio, and he testified to the friar's powers. Later del Fante wrote a major book about the priest entitled *Per la Storia (For History)*, in which he gathered his own testimonies and those of others.

At the time of his conversion, something happened that confirmed del Fante definitively in his faith and put a seal on it. His young wife was expecting a baby, and the father-to-be was very anxious because she had been unable to breast feed her other two children. One day del Fante was at the point of leaving Padre Pio, and he wanted to recommend his wife and her problem to the priest. Del Fante was about to speak when Padre Pio interjected, "Will your wife have milk for this little one?" Del Fante was amazed because this was precisely what was on his mind at that moment. Padre Pio assured him that everything would be all right, and it was!

"Padre Pio! Give me a sign!"

Auré Caviggioli, an antique dealer from Monte Carlo, had been away from the Church for a long time. One day he went to the Rome-Termini station and, without knowing why, bought a ticket for Foggia. During the journey he dozed off, and when he woke up, he became aware of a strong perfume, but could not identify its source.

On his arrival in Foggia, he took the bus for San Giovanni Rotondo and checked into the hotel. Next morning, on his way to Padre Pio's Mass, he was aware of the same perfume he had smelled on the train. During the celebration of Mass, he was fascinated by the priest's presence. He wanted to get near, but the crowd was dense. The next day, thanks to some Brothers, he was able to get close to Padre Pio who asked him, "What do you want?" Caviggioli was embarrassed for a moment, and then he remembered that one of his grand-daughters, living in Switzerland, had a brain tumor, so he recommended her to Padre Pio's prayers. Padre Pio advised him to go home because the child had been cured. The cure, in fact, had been immediate and complete, so much so that the doctors would not take their fees, as they concluded they had done nothing in this case.

This excited Caviggioli's curiosity, and he went back several times to San Giovanni Rotondo to meet Padre Pio and make his confession to him. But a certain fear held him back. Two years passed and he decided to make Padre Pio a gift of a painting of the Virgin Mary carrying the child Jesus, the work of a painter of the sixteenth century. A friend who came to look at it asked Caviggioli how much the painting was worth. Caviggioli answered that it was worth millions! But during the night Padre Pio came to him in a dream and, looking at him very severely, said, "What are you talking about? You only paid 25,000 lire for that painting!" When the antique dealer woke up, he recalled that, in fact, this was the price he had paid a Jewish man for it, and that man was later deported during World War II.

When Caviggioli went to San Giovanni Rotondo, he presented the painting to Padre Pio who asked him, "What did you dream last night, you rogue?" and burst out laughing. The dealer told the priest his dream and he too laughed.

Even on this occasion, however, Padre Pio would not hear Caviggioli's confession. Back at his hotel, alone and looking at the monastery, the antique dealer cried out, "Listen! Padre Pio! Give me a sign that I may know when to come to confession." To his utter amazement, Caviggioli had hardly finished the sentence when Padre Pio appeared before him, took him by the hand, and then disappeared. Caviggioli was filled with fear and was quite stunned by this. Next day the priest heard the man's confession and apologized for having scared him by appearing at the hotel!

A voice in the night said, "Get up and go to Padre Pio."

Luigi Rago, from Salerno, although married and a father, had the habit of looking for a good time with attractive women when he was away from home on business. One night in 1960, he was with a woman in a hotel in Foggia when he heard, interiorly, a strong, stern voice ordering him in no uncertain terms, "Get up and go find Padre Pio!"

Rago, who since his youth had given up the Church and religious practice, had no idea who Padre Pio might be. But faced with this strange and imperative command, he felt that he had no option but to obey. He got up and dressed. To those who asked him where he was going at this hour, he replied, "I am going to see Padre Pio at San Giovanni Rotondo." At two o'clock in the morning he was at the door of the church where a crowd had gathered to attend Padre Pio's Mass. Rago joined them and went close to the altar where the celebration was to take place. When Padre Pio arrived, Rago felt a kind of electric shock go through his body, and he followed every detail of the Mass, which he saw as an enthralling show. In spite of all this, he did not dare approach the friar. From that time, however, he felt a great desire to go to church and pray. Whenever he had occasion to be in Foggia, he always went to San Giovanni Rotondo to attend Padre Pio's Mass. Back in Salerno he adopted the habit of going to a church to pray before its painting of the Madonna. He ended up by breaking off the relationship he had with the woman who was his mistress.

Yet his soul was still far from being peaceful and serene. His sins weighed heavily on him. He went back one day to San Giovanni Rotondo and asked Padre Pio to hear his confession. "What's this?" Padre Pio demanded. "You have been away from the Church for many, many years. You did not pray, and you gave your soul to the devil! Get out of here!"

Rago was deeply ashamed but did not lose heart. Padre Pio did not forget him. He appeared to Rago in a dream, spreading his special perfume around, gave him spiritual comfort, and told him of a good priest he should see. Rago went off to find the priest and made a general confession. From that moment he came back to the Church, was at peace with himself, and reconciled with his family and friends. He wanted to be reconciled with Padre Pio too, so he went to the priest and said, "Father, the last time I was here you chased me away." Padre Pio replied, "And who can say anything against you now, my son?" This was the beginning of a spiritual friendship that had an influence on everyone who knew Rago.

A trap that worked

A trader from Genoa had to visit Foggia to negotiate an oil sale. One of his friends, who knew he had been away from the Church for a long time, planned to lay a trap for him! The friend asked the trader to make a little detour to San Giovanni Rotondo to deliver a letter to Padre Pio, hoping that his friend would meet the priest. The man accepted this task and took the letter. At Foggia he boarded the bus for San Giovanni Rotondo. Tired out by such a long journey, he had but one thought in mind—to get rid of the letter as quickly as possible. When a Brother opened the door, the trader gave him the letter and said he wanted an immediate reply because he had to be on his way. He was invited into the sacristy to wait until Padre Pio would come down to give him an answer. The trader waited a few minutes in the sacristy and began to grow impatient. Padre Pio arrived but made no impression on his visitor. The priest approached, looked him straight in the eye, and asked, "Now you, what do you want?" The man answered that he just wanted a reply to the letter. "Ah, yes," Padre Pio said, "the letter! But what about you? Don't you want to go to confession?" The man admitted that he had not practiced his religion for a very long time. Padre Pio asked him, "How long is it since your last confession?" "I was seven years old," said the trader. The priest looked at him in such a way that it seemed he saw into his soul, and said, "How long do you intend living this disgusting kind of life?"

In a flash he saw how his life had been lived without God, so he repented, went to confession, and was filled with joy! He had gone to the monastery rather unwillingly as a favor to his friend, intending to be done with this obligation as quickly as possible. He stayed for another week, fascinated by Padre Pio, attending his Mass and receiving communion at his hands. The trap set by the trader's friend had worked perfectly!

A spate of chain conversions

Luisa Vairo was living in London when she made a visit to San Giovanni Rotondo in September 1925. She told the story of her own conversion and that of others linked to it.

This woman lived without giving any thought to religion. She enjoyed a life of pleasure, yet found no satisfaction in it. It was during this time of stress that she was shaken by something that happened to one of her friends. He was converted, thanks to Padre Pio. The story this friend told her impressed her so much that she decided to meet this famous Capuchin.

One day she arrived at San Giovanni and experienced a strange feeling when she saw the poverty and destitution of the countryside and the monastery. (With all the changes that have taken place since 1925, this is hard to imagine today!) What a contrast with the drawing rooms of London! The woman's first reaction was that of repugnance, and she wanted to escape as quickly as possible. She began, however, to feel a kind of attraction to the simplicity, the serenity, and the tranquility of the atmosphere. She was perplexed and terrified at the thought of meeting a priest who knew and saw everything and lived with the suffering of the stigmata. She became aware of the abyss that separated her pleasure-seeking way of life from this mysterious world, and she began to sob uncontrollably, disturbing those around her in the little church!

Padre Pio arrived and came over to her as if he had known her all his life. "Don't be so upset, Madam! God's mercy is infinite. Jesus died on the cross for sinners."

Madam Vairo replied immediately, "I want to go to confession, Father."

"Be at peace, Madam," the priest answered. "Now is not the moment."

"I don't even know what to say," she replied.

Padre Pio advised her, "Come back this afternoon at three o'clock, and I will hear your confession. Now, go and freshen up, then come and find me. If you don't know what to say, I will do the talking for you!"

The woman did exactly as she was told, but her mind was agitated and in a state of utter confusion, to the extent that she could not prepare properly for her confession. When she came back to Padre Pio, he took the initiative and enumerated all the sins she had ever committed, giving the place, the time, and the circumstances of each one until she went pale as she listened. Padre Pio omitted one sin and asked her, "Is there anything else you can recall?" The penitent was fully aware of this particular that sin she had committed. She wondered if she should admit to it or not. Finally, she decided to acknowledge it. Radiant, Padre Pio cried out, "That's what I was waiting for!" He then absolved her from all her sins.

Madam Vairo, now forgiven, felt like a new person. Not only did she want to spend more time with the priest who had given her new life, but she imposed a severe penance on herself to expiate her sins. One day she decided to walk barefoot to the monastery in freezing rain and sleet. She arrived soaked through and with bleeding feet. When Padre Pio saw her in this state, he told her that this was a rather heavy penance to undertake, then he added, "But this water is not really wet!" Madam Vairo's clothes were dried on the spot!

And that is not the end. Madam Vairo had a son who was, as she had been, away from the Church. In the fervor of her newfound life, she wrote to him telling the wonderful story of her conversion and her enthusiasm for Padre Pio. She invited her son to join her at San Giovanni Rotondo. He wanted nothing to do with all this and replied that he would never come, not even out of curiosity. Padre Pio urged the mother to persevere in prayer for her son, assuring her that he too would one day be converted.

Some time later, a friend brought her a newspaper with the story that the ship her son had been on had been sunk and that many passengers had drowned. She was convinced that her son was among them, and she was plunged into a state of deep distress and hopelessness. When Padre Pio learned the reason for her anguish, he asked, "Who told you that your son was dead and has reduced you to this state?" She replied, "Who can tell me if he is alive?" The priest recollected himself in prayer and declared, "Thanks be to God! Your son is alive, and he can be found in such and such a place." Padre Pio pinpointed the place with precision. The mother wrote immediately to the address at the same time as the survivor was writing to reassure her of his safety. Their letters crossed, and the son was mystified as to how his mother could have known where he was staying. This intrigued him so much that he went to San Giovanni Rotondo to clear up the mystery.

When he arrived, his mother asked him to fast in preparation for confession and to receive Holy Communion from Padre Pio. The young man agreed to do this then excused himself to go to the marketplace, promising to return shortly. While he was out, he bought two eggs, which he guzzled down, followed by a bunch of grapes. He then returned to his mother in the sacristy. When Padre Pio arrived, Madam Vairo introduced her son saying, "Father, this is the child I spoke to you about." Padre Pio looked at him somewhat ironically, saying, "What a fraud! What a little liar!" and turning to the woman said, "You believe, don't you, my poor woman, that he has been fasting?" The young man wanted to intervene and ask the priest, "Why are you treating me in this way? You don't even know me!" But Padre Pio broke in saying, "Do you still want to insist that you were fasting? What about the eggs and the bunch of grapes you have eaten?" The young man gave in, saying, "Father, forgive me. I believe!" He, in his turn, became a convert.

Called in his sleep

One night a young engineer from Bologna, who had been away from the Church for years, dreamed of Padre Pio. During the dream, the friar gazed at the engineer for a long time and then disappeared after saying, "It is fortunate for you that you could sustain my scrutiny!" The young man had no idea who Padre Pio was and had never even heard of him. The dream intrigued the engineer very much so he decided to make some inquiries. He heard someone mentioning the priest. His feelings were very mixed. He had a great desire to meet this man and, at the same time, his conscience pricked him. He wanted to come out of his spiritual dilemma but did not feel the inner strength to do so. So he sank back into his lethargy and eight years went by.

It took a catastrophe—an earthquake that shook Bologna —to wake him out of his apathy. The engineer decided to visit Padre Pio and took the train to San Giovanni Rotondo. After traveling several kilometers, he felt ill and had to return home. To explain this inconvenience, he wrote to Padre Pio. The priest replied through a confrere, counseling him to be patient, to pray and engage in charitable work until the right moment came along. Some time later, after gathering information from some followers of Padre Pio, he again went off to San Giovanni Rotondo. When he saw Padre Pio at the monastery, he recognized him. The priest looked exactly like the friar in his dream eight years earlier. The engineer fell on his knees, weeping, and managed to blurt out, "I have known of your reputation for holiness for eight years!" Padre Pio replied, "What good has it done you? You have lived as you wished! Change your life, my son!" This time the engineer readily accepted Padre Pio's advice. He went to confession and received absolution. Utterly changed, he returned to Bologna and told the story to his family and friends.

The return of the lost artist

Professor Felice Checcacci from Genoa was a writer and composer of some renown and a proverbial "lost sheep!" For about forty years he had lived in Asia, had given up his

Christian identity, and had embraced other traditions to the point that he believed Christianity to be an offshoot of Brahmanism and Buddhism.

On his return to Italy, he had occasion to read the work of Alberto del Fante on Padre Pio, *Dal dubbio alla fede* (*From Doubt to Faith*), and another book by the same author, *Per la Storia* (*For History*). These books disturbed him deeply. One night he dreamed that Padre Pio said to him, "Come and see me!" He did not pay any heed. Two or three months later the priest appeared to him in another dream, saying, "I waited for you, but you did not come!" Still, the professor was unaffected.

Some time later, when he was lying awake, the professor saw Padre Pio come into his room and approach the bed, saying, "If you can't come to see me, at least write!" Checcacci was left in no doubt about the presence of Padre Pio. He saw him, heard him speak, and was terrified! He got out of bed to speak to the priest, but he had already disappeared.

The next morning Checcacci wrote to Padre Pio, asking him for peace of soul. Two days later, in the afternoon, the professor felt his body shake from head to toe, and at the same time he heard an interior voice say to him, "Faith is not up for discussion. You either accept it blindly or you reject it. There is no in-between. You must make the choice." Suddenly a great light filled his soul, he found his faith again and bore witness to this by living in great peace of mind.

The fasting laborer

At San Martino in Pensilis lived a laborer called Andrea Bacile. This man never went to church, never received the sacraments, and called himself as an atheist. He had no use for religion. He was married and had children, loved his wife and family very much, and looked after them well. However, he did not always agree with his wife.

One night they had a violent argument, and he went to bed in a foul mood. He was about to put out the bedroom light when, suddenly, he saw Padre Pio standing in front of him. It was not difficult for him to identify the friar from the many photographs and drawings he had seen of this priest. Without hesitation Bacile asked if he could go to confession. Padre Pio replied, "No!" and disappeared.

The next day Bacile reconciled with his wife and, fasting, set out on the road to San Giovanni Rotondo. It took him three days to reach the monastery, where he arrived exhausted, very hungry, and wanting to go immediately to confession. After giving the laborer absolution, Padre Pio said, without knowing anything about this man, "Now go and eat!"

Justified harshness

A woman from England traveled to San Giovanni Rotondo to go to Padre Pio for confession, but when he saw her behind the screen, he violently closed the grill, saying to her, "I have no time for someone like you!" It is not difficult to imagine how stunned she was—as well as those who witnessed what had happened.

Why did Padre Pio treat this penitent so badly? Some of those close to the priest felt it was their duty to tell him that this woman had come a long distance to receive absolution. But their plea fell on deaf ears! This went on for twenty days. The Englishwoman went each day to the confessional, and each day she was sent away. Finally, Padre Pio decided to hear her confession. When she complained to him about having to wait so long, he said, "How can you be so blind? Instead of moaning about my severity, ask yourself how the mercy of God could possibly come to you after so many years of sacrilege. Do you realize what a terrible thing you have done? Whoever commits a sacrilege is condemned out of hand and cannot be saved without a special grace, which can only come through someone close to God. Although you were in mortal sin, you went to Holy Communion with your mother and husband, year after year, just to keep up appearances."

Padre Pio's instant revelation of this woman's past profoundly affected her. She repented of her past, went to confession, and, at last, received absolution. Her life was completely changed, and she lived her Christian commitment fully to make up for her past sins.

A murder was planned but . . .

A man who one day came to Padre Pio was the type of hard, cold criminal who will stop at nothing. This individual wanted to get rid of his wife, but in such a way that his crime would be cloaked with a motive of piety.

Under the pretext of going to see Padre Pio, the man brought his wife with him to San Giovanni Rotondo where he planned to kill her in a most diabolical way. On arriving at the monastery, he went through the Capuchins' church to the sacristy. Padre Pio was there, talking to some people. When the priest saw the man, he left the group abruptly, went to the man, and began to push him violently toward the door, shouting at the top of his voice, "Get out! Get out! Don't you know it is forbidden to stain your hands with blood? Get out!"

The unfortunate man was dumbfounded and, livid with rage, bolted out of the church, to the astonishment of everyone there. The strong words and behavior of Padre Pio, however, made such an impression on the man that he could not get a wink of sleep all night. He began to understand the horror of what he was planning and, touched by grace, woke up a different man in the morning.

He went to the monastery, and this time Padre Pio received him with great tenderness, heard his confession, and gave him absolution. To crown everything, Padre Pio asked him before he left, "You have always wanted children, haven't you?" The man thought to himself, "Blast! How could the priest have known that?" He had never mentioned this to anyone! The priest went on, "Do not offend God anymore, and you will have a son." A year later the man returned to Padre Pio to celebrate the confirmation of his conversion and his son's baptism.

CHAPTER 4

A Penetrating Gaze

Many who came to Padre Pio were taken aback and astounded by the revelations he made to them about their lives, both past and present. Sometimes he even revealed future events, and these always took place! It could be said that Padre Pio read the destiny of individuals like an open book.

How can these things be explained? As far as I am concerned, I think that, in these cases, Padre Pio was able to reach into the individual lives of those who came to him because he could see them surrounded with God's powerful light. This helped him to adapt his treatment of souls to the way he thought best, according to his conscience. Moreover, he told one of his confreres that he dealt with souls in the way the Lord showed him to.

In the following pages, I offer some stories of this kind. Others have already been told about the conversion of some of the people mentioned.

Like a page in a diary

A priest set out on a long journey to visit Padre Pio and make his confession to him. He had to change trains at Bologna and wait a very long time for his connection. By this time he was rather tired and went to a hotel room where he fell fast asleep and only woke up at three in the afternoon!

He had not been able to say his Mass because at that time Mass had to be celebrated in the morning. It was an unintentional mistake to which he did not attach a great deal of importance. But Padre Pio did not see it this way! When the priest arrived, Padre Pio asked him, after his confession and absolution, "My brother! Have you perhaps forgotten something?" The priest replied, "No, Father."

Padre Pio suggested that he take time to search his soul, which he did thoroughly and still came up with nothing. Then Padre Pio said to him, "My son, you arrived at Bologna railway station yesterday morning. The churches were closed, but instead of waiting until they opened, you went to a hotel and fell asleep until three in the afternoon, and therefore you were too late to celebrate Mass. I know you did not do this on purpose, but it was an act of negligence that hurt our Lord."

By giving this priest a summary, like a page from a diary, of all that had happened the preceding day, Padre Pio wanted to drive home to the priest the importance of the Mass in the life of a man consecrated to the priesthood.

"Call him Pio! Call him Francis!"

An officer in the carabinieri had no time for Padre Pio. He did not think highly of the priest and took every opportunity to put him down. One day, however, the officer decided to meet the priest in person and went to San Giovanni Rotondo. When Padre Pio saw the officer, he asked point-blank, "Why do you tell all these cock and bull stories about me when you have never even met me? Look and see first, judge for yourself, and then say what you want!"

The officer was won over, as he began to understand and appreciate Padre Pio. Some time later he brought some news to the priest, "Father, my wife is expecting a baby! What should we name it?"

Padre Pio replied immediately, "Name him Pio."

"And what if it's a girl?"

Padre Pio repeated, very clearly, "I told you to call him Pio!"

A boy was born and the couple named him Pio.

Two years later, this officer came back to see Padre Pio and to tell him that his wife was pregnant again. "So what name should we give this time?" the officer asked.

Padre Pio answered, "Call him Francis."

The officer raised some doubts, "Father, we had a boy last time, but this sort of thing does not necessarily come in a series!"

Padre Pio cried out, "Man of little faith!"

The officer's wife gave birth to a boy, and the couple named him Francis.

"He's crazy!"

A friend of mine, a doctor, went to Padre Pio one day, just at the same time as the famous actor Carlo Campanini and a veterinarian from Bologna. Padre Pio told Campanini to put his son in a home. Then Padre Pio looked at an x-ray of the veterinarian's son, whom doctors' suspected of having a brain tumor. The priest told the man not to worry, but to take his son back to Bologna, assuring him that his son was fine.

All this came true. At the time, however, my friend, the doctor, thought it all a bit risky. "He's crazy!" he said to himself. He was even more convinced of this when Padre Pio came up to him and put his hand on his head and said, "You are a bit absentminded, aren't you?" The doctor said to himself, "Now I know for sure that he is completely crazy!" The doctor had, in fact, an excellent memory, so good that he could remember all the names of the many types of medicine, some of which had very strange names indeed! This is why he knew it was out of the question that he could be forgetful.

After his visit to Padre Pio, he remembered that before going to see the priest, he had gone into a local bar for a coffee. He had no small change to pay for the drink, so he had handed the waiter a ten-thousand-lire bill. The waiter had put the change down on the counter, but the doctor had forgotten to pick it up. When the doctor recalled this, he went back to the bar, but the barman pretended he knew nothing about the forgotten change. The waiter said he had given the doctor his change and that was that! My friend tried to explain as well as he could that he had not taken the change, but there was nothing to be done. In the end he said to himself, "It's not Padre Pio who is crazy, but me, since I ended up paying ten thousand lire for a thirty-lire cup of coffee!"

A fifty-year-long misunderstanding

One of the first photographers of Padre Pio's stigmata, in its first stages, was a man called Modesto Vinelli. He made copies of his photographs and sold them everywhere to make Padre Pio known. One day he arrived at Rodi Garganico and met a man who wanted to hear nothing about Padre Pio. A rather heated discussion followed that led to violence. Vinelli defended the priest against the insults, curses, and blasphemies of the other man. After a while, Vinelli gave way to his anger and began punching and kicking the man. The man was injured, and Vinelli was arrested and jailed for forty days.

When he was released from jail, he went to Padre Pio and said, "Father, I was sent to prison because of you!" Padre Pio asked, "Because of me? What did you do?" Vinelli told him all that had happened at Rodi Garganico. The priest advised Vinelli to be patient with those who did not think along the same lines, and especially that he, Vinelli, had to keep his fists to himself, adding, "Modesto, remember we still have fifty years ahead of us!"

What did Padre Pio mean by these words? Probably the following: "We must be patient with those who do not think as we do because, with time, the truth will come out, and we have fifty years ahead of us for that."

Unfortunately, Vinelli failed to understand the priest's words in this way. He thought Padre Pio was telling him that he, personally, had only fifty years to live!

Every year, on September 20, Vinelli went to the monastery for the anniversary of Padre Pio's stigmata, and as the years went by he heard the priest tell him how many years remained. On the twenty-fifth year, as usual on this date, Vinelli went to see Padre Pio who said to him, "Modesto, twenty-five years have passed!"

The photographer found some consolation in the fact that if twenty-five years had gone, it was equally true that twenty-five years remained. He began to worry, however, and his anxiety only increased with the passing years. On September 20, 1968, two days before Padre Pio's death, Vinelli went to see the priest. This time Padre Pio said, "Modesto, the fifty years are over!" Vinelli was very upset, nearing his breaking point because he thought Padre Pio was telling him *he* would die. The shock was so intense that Modesto nearly collapsed. Someone explained to him that the priest was speaking of his own death, which he foresaw as imminent, and not Vinelli's.

In fact, on the night of September 23, 1968, Padre Pio died. Despite his sadness over losing such a dear friend, Vinelli was relieved that the misunderstanding was cleared up! He lived another fifteen years, and he died on March 2, 1983.

"No! You will forget it!"

Among the many people who came to see Padre Pio was Archbishop Marcel Lefebvre who, later clinging stubbornly to Catholic Tradition, as he called it, questioned the authority of Vatican II and was removed from office by Pope Paul VI.

The archbishop had a meeting with Padre Pio in the presence of Professor Bruno Rabajotti. This witness reported that at a particular moment Padre Pio looked at Lefebvre very sternly and said, "Never cause discord among your brothers, and always practice the rule of obedience, above all, when it seems to you that the errors of those in authority are all the more serious. There is no other road than that of obedience, especially for those of us who have made this vow."

Padre Pio could give this advice because he had the experience of having to obey some rather questionable orders himself. His attitude was to put this in God's hands because

God would find a way for truth to triumph. It seems that Archbishop Lefebvre did not see things in quite the same way, even if he did respond to Padre Pio with "I will remember that, Father." Padre Pio looked at the archbishop intensely, and, seeing what would soon happen, said, "No! You will forget it! You will tear apart the community of the faithful, oppose the will of your superiors, and even go against the orders of the Pope himself, and this will happen quite soon. You will forget the promise you made here today, and the whole Church will be hurt by you. Don't set yourself up as a judge. Don't take powers that do not belong to you, and do not consider yourself as the voice of God's people, as God already speaks to them. Do not sow discord and dissension. However, I know this is what you will do!"

Unfortunately, the truth of Padre Pio's prophecy is obvious to everyone.

Don't play games with suffering

Professor Bruno Rabajotti tells how, one day, a group made up of two laymen, a religious from the monastery at San Giovanni, and a priest decided to play a rather bad joke on Padre Pio. They persuaded a man of about thirty-five to pretend he was paralyzed.

They went together to the monastery and waited in the parlor for Padre Pio on the pretense that they had brought someone for a cure. It was a Friday, the day on which Padre Pio's sufferings were particularly intense. At times, the priest was in such agony that he could not come down to the church for Mass or confessions. He was called to the parlor and arrived there with great difficulty.

When he reached the doorway, he immediately looked at the false paralytic and came toward him saying, "You are here pretending to be ill, but your real illness is in your soul. It has wounds you cannot begin to imagine! Understand this: You cannot play games with suffering. God does not will it. The illness you feigned today will strike your family. You brought on this misfortune. You wanted suffering!" Having said this, Padre Pio looked at him for a few moments and then went away.

The young man was very shaken by these words and went home as quickly as he could. When he got there, he learned that his brother had been hit by a car. His brother had been taken immediately to the hospital where he was given emergency treatment, but the doctors could do nothing about his injuries: he would be paralyzed for life.

The following Sunday there was a conference at the monastery, and Padre Pio was present. When it ended, the priest got up to leave. He saw the false paralytic in the crowd. The young man threw himself at Padre Pio's feet, crying, "Have mercy on me, Father, for I have sinned. My brother was not the one who sinned. Cure him and let God do to me what he wants!" Padre Pio replied, "It is not for me to grant you pardon, but go ask it of the priest who went along with your charade. And may you be as worthy of what you ask as you deserved what happened to you."

The following week, as he was passing a line of people waiting for confession, Padre Pio noticed the same man curled up in a corner, praying. Usually, Padre Pio did not stop during such situations, but he hesitated for a moment, puzzled. He went toward the unfortunate man, laid his hands on him, and whispered something in his ear.

Later, it was revealed that the false paralytic's brother had been cured in an extraordinary way, and the unfortunate joker became one of Padre Pio's most fervent spiritual sons.

The pictures did not cause the blasphemy

In 1926 a bus driver from San Severo took pilgrims to the grotto at Monte Sant'Angelo. This had become a shrine to St. Michael the Archangel, who had appeared there and had been venerated for centuries.

The driver, a follower of Padre Pio, attended Mass with the pilgrims and then went for a walk around the town. He came to a bakery where they were making biscuits, a specialty of the area, and he went in to buy some to share with the pilgrims. When he received the bag, he realized he had received only half the amount he had ordered. This irritated him so much that he let slip a blasphemy! He went back to the pilgrims and drove them to San Giovanni Rotondo where they went to Padre Pio for confession. When the priest had finished hearing their confessions, he turned to the driver and asked, "And you, my son? Don't you want even a blessing?" The driver replied that he really had nothing to confess and his conscience was at peace. Padre Pio insisted, so the driver went into the confessional. The priest asked him what he had been doing all day. The driver told him he had been to Mass with the pilgrims at Sant'Angelo and that he had bought some pictures. The priest said to him, "But it was not the pictures that made you blaspheme, rather something you ate!" The man remembered the blasphemy he had uttered on leaving the bakery. Padre Pio went on: "You also insulted the cart driver who did not keep to his right!" All this was true.

Words were unnecessary

The next two incidents happened to me, so I am a prime witness. For a long time I had been worried about a spiritual problem that I could not put right because I did not know its causes. I had never spoken to anyone about this. One day I got the opportunity I needed to talk about it.

A friend who lived at San Giovanni Rotondo, well known to the Capuchins there, invited me to stay in his home and arranged for me to meet Padre Pio. I was greeted by Father Venanzio, one of the priests who scheduled Padre Pio's visits. He brought me in, saying, "Wait here. Padre Pio will not be long, but this is Friday, when the wounds bleed more profusely. He has gone to the kitchen to wash." While waiting, I went over in my mind all that I wanted to say to present my situation in the most precise and clearest way possible.

Shortly afterward, I saw Padre Pio coming down the corridor. As he approached me, and without giving me time to speak, he whispered in my ear, "This is the reason for your situation!" and he summed it up in a single sentence.

Although thirty years have gone by since he said this to me, I remember it word for word as if it were yesterday! I was completely thrown by this. There was no need to talk because the priest had gone right to the heart of the problem and found its cause. After this Padre Pio walked away, then came back and repeated what he had said so that there would be no doubt in my mind. He started to return to his cell and, halfway there, he turned round and said, "Where are you saying Mass tomorrow?" Still a bit shaken by all that had happened, I answered vaguely, "I don't know Father."

"You don't want to come here to say it?"

I replied, "Yes, yes, Father! I will say Mass here!"

Padre Pio finished by saying, "Yes, come! You must say Mass here tomorrow." He went on up the stairs and disappeared along the corridor.

When I returned to my friend's house, everyone noticed I was deep in thought. They asked, "What's the matter with you, Father Cataneo?" I told them Padre Pio had read my soul and solved my problem. When they heard this, they exclaimed, "So, what people say about him is true. You know, here in San Giovanni, we hear so many things, but if *you* tell us that this is what happened, then it is true!" I said to them, "You can be sure that it is really true. I am irrefutable proof of that."

"This spiritual life."

At one time, priests who did not reside in San Giovanni Rotondo could line up to go to Padre Pio for confession, one priest after every five lay penitents. I wanted to speak to him on certain matters but realized it was now much more difficult to have a private talk with him than when I had first met him. So many people wanted to get near Padre Pio that the crowds had to be organized and directed.

I thought the best thing to do, if I wanted to go to confession to him, was to make use of the arrangement offered to nonresident priests and speak my heart to him in the confessional. I was aware that many people who wanted to go to confession were, perhaps, in greater need than I, so I decided to make a thorough preparation so that I would not waste Padre Pio's time.

I made my examination of conscience in the bus from Foggia on my way to San Giovanni Rotondo. I recall that, on a bend in the road where the town came into view, I finished my examination, thinking to myself, "This spiritual life, what an adventure! It's like walking on glass!" Then my mind turned to other things. The bus dropped me off at the Capuchin monastery, and I went to the chapel and waited in line where Padre Pio was hearing confessions. When my turn came, I opened my heart to him. Padre Pio gave me the answers I was waiting for, and I received his absolution. Just as I was about to get up off my knees, he turned to me, with a twinkle in his eye, and said, "This spiritual life, what an adventure! It's like walking on glass, isn't it?" He had read my thoughts even before I reached San Giovanni Rotondo, and he repeated them word for word, although I had already forgotten them!

I was astonished but at the same time received great encouragement from this reflection of his because it pointed to the difficulties we meet in all spiritual life and the temptation to give up. In repeating what I had thought, Padre Pio was certainly saying to me, "You think you have difficulties? What should I say about mine? Courage!"

A petty thief is caught

Among the people who flocked to Padre Pio, there were always some who wanted to snatch some relic from him out of devotion or fanatic zeal. He could not stand this as it surrounded him with the kind of aura of sanctity that he detested. He reacted every time it happened, and sometimes harshly, such was his character. Someone pointed out to him that this response could upset people, but Padre Pio showed his torn habit and slashed Franciscan cord and said, "And if I don't react, where will it all end?"

One evening, after praying the Office, he went to the garden with some friends and doctors from Casa Sollievo della

Sofferenza (the House for the Relief of Suffering), a hospital he had founded. Cosimo Iadanza, a fellow countryman of Padre Pio, was in the group. The priest had forgotten his handkerchief. He called Cosimo and said, "Here, Cosimo, would you take the key to my cell and fetch me a handkerchief? I need one!" Cosimo took the key and went to the friar's cell. He found a handkerchief but could not resist the temptation to take something else to keep as a relic. He went back to the garden, looking innocent of the whole affair, and gave Padre Pio the handkerchief. The priest gave him a strange look and said, "Go back this minute to my room, and replace what you have put in your pocket." Cosimo blushed. He really believed that he could get away with taking the relic because no one had seen him. He had not reckoned with Padre Pio's penetrating mind!

He smelled a rat!

One of Padre Pio's American benefactors came to San Giovanni Rotondo to see the priest. They had hardly met when Padre Pio pushed him aside brusquely and said, "Go away! I do not know you!" The poor man was upset and wondered why he was being treated in this way.

The benefactor went off to find Father Alberto D'Apolito, who lived at San Severo. He thought that if the priest came with him, Padre Pio might recognize him and receive them both. Father D'Apolito thought that if Padre Pio had treated the American that badly, then there was something not quite right. He smelled a rat! (In fact, the American had a mistress!) Father D'Apolito, however, accompanied his visitor to San Giovanni Rotondo, warning the man, "You'll see! The minute

Padre Pio sees us, he will chase both of us away!" Sure enough, as soon as Padre Pio saw the man accompanied by Father D'Apolito, he shouted, "So you needed someone to plead for you! Go away, both of you!"

So they left. When Father D'Apolito heard that the American was going to Assisi and Padua, he advised him to go to confession at one of these shrines. The American did as the priest said. Before leaving Italy to return to America, the traveler wanted to go back to San Giovanni Rotondo to meet Padre Pio. Again, Father Alberto went with him. This time, Padre Pio received the man with great kindness, thanked him for his generosity, made a few requests, embraced, and blessed him, saying, "When you return to America, make sure you are a good Christian. You understand?" The man promised, but later on, because of weakness, fell back into his old ways.

The following year the American wanted to return to San Giovanni Rotondo, and he asked Padre Pio, through Father D'Apolito, if he might return. Padre Pio replied, "No!"

Time went by and eventually the benefactor ended the relationship with his mistress, and devoted himself to his wife and family. Again, he asked Padre Pio if he could see him. This time the priest said, "Yes!" The man, who arrived just in time to receive Padre Pio's blessing, died very soon afterward.

Answering a sealed letter

A parish priest who saw so many of his people go to Padre Pio was resentful of this and wanted to trap Padre Pio by sending him a letter. In it he asked the friar a question. He sealed the letter, gave it to one of his parishioners who was going to San Giovanni Rotondo, and insisted that the parishioner personally place the letter into the hands of Padre Pio and wait for a reply. The man agreed to do this and set out for San Giovanni Rotondo with a parish group. When he arrived, Padre Pio welcomed the man with all the others and then singled him out and approached him, saying, "Take out the letter you have in your pocket, and write down this reply on the envelope." The messenger brought out the letter and, with his big handwriting, wrote down the reply dictated by the friar.

When he arrived home, the man went to the parish priest and told him that Padre Pio had replied to his letter without even opening it! The priest read the reply the parishioner had written on the sealed envelope, and to his astonishment saw that this was the exact answer to the question he had asked Padre Pio! Obviously it was not easy to ensnare Padre Pio!

"Padre Pio sent us."

It is well known that Pope Benedict XV held Padre Pio in high esteem. In his entourage, however, some considered the priest to be an imposter. Among them was a bishop who believed it was his duty to warn the Pope against Padre Pio. Benedict XV pointed out to this bishop that before taking sides against the friar he should meet Padre Pio and get to know all about him. The Pope advised the bishop to go to San Giovanni Rotondo and see things for himself and discover the truth about Padre Pio.

When the bishop arrived at Foggia, he was greeted by two Capuchins. They explained that Padre Pio had sent them to accompany him to San Giovanni Rotondo. Astonished, the bishop told them that no one knew of his visit, least of all Padre Pio! The two Capuchins told him that Padre Pio had given them the description of a bishop, sent by the Pope, instructing them to accompany him to San Giovanni Rotondo. The bishop was very embarrassed by all this. What should he do? Should he go or not? He realized that if the priest already knew of his coming, he was likely to know also what he had said against him to the Pope. To save face, the bishop decided to make up the excuse of having a rather urgent appointment to keep, and he returned to Rome.

"*Coward!*"

It was a well-known fact that Padre Pio was not intimidated by anything or anyone. He was very forthright and frank in what he had to say, and even, at times, harsh, when his conscience called for it. I think this behavior sprang from the fact that being so deeply rooted in God, he could deal with people in great freedom.

No one could apply to him what Jesus said to his disciples one day: "If someone disowns me before men, the Son of Man will disown him before the Father." Jesus wanted his spiritual sons to behave like him. The following incident should be understood in this context.

One of his spiritual sons in Rome had the habit of raising his hat when passing a church to honor the presence of the Blessed Sacrament there. One day he was out with friends who were more interested in the trifles and things of the world. They passed by a church, and he was ashamed to raise his hat in their company. At that moment he heard a loud cry in his ear, "Coward!" Later, when he returned to San Giovanni Rotondo and met Padre Pio, the priest said to him, "Watch out! This time you just got a reprimand, but next time you'll get your ears boxed!"

"You will die in eight days!"

To tell a young policeman in full vigor that he would die in eight days was not a pleasant task, but, because of his gift of foresight, Padre Pio felt compelled to do so. He tried to be as tactful and gentle as possible.

One day when putting away vestments in the sacristy after Mass, Padre Pio turned to one of the two policemen posted at the door to protect him from the crowds. "When I have finished my thanksgiving prayers," he said, "follow me to my cell. I want to speak with you." The young policeman was delighted, but when he was alone with the priest, his delight turned to sadness. Padre Pio said to him, "Listen my son, in about eight days you will be going to your father's house, and there you will die."

The young man did not want to believe this and told Padre Pio that he was in perfect health. But the priest would not be put off and added, "Don't worry! You will feel even better in eight days. What is life anyway but a pilgrimage. We are on a journey, my son." Padre Pio advised the policeman to ask for some time off to arrange his affairs. The young man asked if he could tell anyone about what had transpired between them. Padre Pio replied, "No! Not at the moment. Wait until you get home."

It was not easy for the young officer to get permission to go home because his chief could not see the necessity for this, and the young man could not tell him of Padre Pio's prophecy.

The priest had to intervene so that the officer could get the permission he needed. At home the policeman told his astonished and unbelieving family what Padre Pio had said. He put his affairs in order, and eight days later he died suddenly.

She did not believe Padre Pio but . . .

Father Constantino Capobianco tells the story that one day, on the train to Rome, he sat down beside a woman traveling with her brother who worked in Public Security. Both were from Pietrelcina. The woman, dressed in black, seemed very upset. After talking with them for a while, the priest learned that they were returning home from San Giovanni Rotondo where they had spoken to Padre Pio and told him of their anxiety about the woman's husband. The husband was a sailor, and they were afraid he had gone down with his cruiser. Padre Pio told the grieving woman and her brother not to worry and to trust in the Lord: "In a few days you will get some good news!" The woman was so convinced that her husband was dead that she did not believe Padre Pio.

A few days after her return to Pietrelcina, she received a telegram from her husband! He told her not to worry, that he was safe. The submarine that had torpedoed the cruiser had picked up the survivors, and he was among them, safe in England. His wife now knew that Padre Pio's words were to be trusted!

Marocchino's goldfinch

At the time when Padre Pio was spiritual director of the monastery at San Giovanni, there was, among the postulants, a young man nicknamed Marocchino. This novice loved the arts and nature.

One day a goldfinch flew in from the garden and got trapped in the corridor running alongside the friars' refectory. When Marocchino saw the bird, he wanted to catch and keep it in a cage for his enjoyment. He went after it, but the bird flew and hopped around from place to place, zigzagging as it went. Eventually it got itself stuck in a corner near the kitchen. Marocchino ran forward to catch it, but at that very moment the bell for prayer rang so he had to give up the chase and go to chapel.

Instead of praying, however, he worked out plans to catch the bird, make the cage, and choose the best place to put it. During supper he kept on thinking about the bird. On leaving the refectory he had only one thought in his head: to catch the bird! Padre Pio, who had been reading the postulant's thoughts during prayer and in the refectory, called the young man over: "You are losing your senses over this bird!" Padre Pio reviewed the postulant's ideas, one by one, that had come to him at prayer and during supper.

Later, Marocchino became known as Father Vittore and he recounted all this to Father Capobianco: "When I heard Padre Pio revealing all my thoughts, one by one, with precision, accuracy, and clarity, leaving nothing uncovered, I was bewildered and stood there with my head bowed like someone protecting himself from a raging storm overhead!"

Answer to a forgotten question

When news got out that Padre Pio had received the stigmata, crowds came running to the monastery at San Giovanni

Rotondo. Among the first were some French priests led by Abbé Benoît, Secretary General of the Institut Catholique in Lille.

He had a problem about which he had been struggling for years without finding a solution, but, with the passage of time, he had forgotten about it. At San Giovanni Rotondo he and the other priests were received by Padre Pio. He did not experience anything special on seeing the friar for the first time. As the French priests were about to leave, they asked Padre Pio to autograph some photos. He willingly did as they asked. When Padre Pio came to Abbé Benoît, however, instead of writing on the photo the Abbé held out, he took the breviary from under the Abbé's arm, flipped through to find a blank page, and wrote down a sentence. When Abbé Benoît read it, he realized that this was the answer to his long-forgotten problem.

He understood then that Padre Pio was not the simple priest he had taken him for but one of those who, gifted by God, read the past of others.

"You are on your last legs!"

Father Teofilo dal Pozzo, Provincial Superior at this particular time, was preaching at the Church of San Eligio in Foggia. Over and above this, he had taken on the task of replacing one of the friars at San Giovanni Rotondo who was away preaching for the month of Mary. Father Teofilo had to drive back and forth in a small car between Foggia and San Giovanni Rotondo.

Through an interior revelation, Padre Pio knew that the Provincial did not have long to live and that he was anxious about the amount of work he had taken on. At the beginning Padre Pio did not say anything, but later he felt it his duty to warn the Provincial. He called Father Teofilo and said, "What on earth are you doing? Do you realize that you are on your last legs?"

The priest did not pay much attention to Padre Pio's words, believing him to be joking. He was, after all, in good health and in full activity. Three or four months later an investigation of stomach pains revealed he had a tumor. Within a month he was dead.

A delayed departure

Father Paolino da Casacalenda, Superior of the monastery when Padre Pio received the stigmata, and later the Provincial Superior, had a sister living in San Giovanni. He went there often, either to visit Padre Pio or to see his sister. On the particular day this incident happened, he was in a great hurry!

After having eaten with his confreres, he noticed Padre Pio leaving without bidding him goodbye. He called over to him, "So, Padre Pio, you are going away without embracing me!" Padre Pio replied, "Reverend Father, you will not be leaving today." Father Paolino assured him that he was most certainly leaving and that the car and driver were waiting for him at his sister's door! Padre Pio simply repeated that he would not be leaving that day, and added that if the Provincial wanted to be embraced even twice that was all right with him, but he would not be leaving that day!

Father Paolino was convinced that Padre Pio was making fun of him, so he took his leave of everyone and went to his sister's house. When he got there, he found the driver working on the car engine. He told the priest it was a minor problem and would not prevent his departure. After time and effort, however, it became obvious the trouble was more serious than the driver thought. It was a job for a mechanic, which meant they could not leave until the next day.

The Provincial went back to the monastery to spend the night, and when Padre Pio saw him, he said, "Well Father! What did I tell you?"

"In fifteen days you will die!"

There was a priest in Mantova who had led an exemplary life, full of virtue. One night Padre Pio appeared to him in a dream, and after congratulating the priest on his good life, announced that it would soon come to an end. Padre Pio told the priest that he would die in fifteen days and that he should use the time well to prepare for a perfect ending to this final stage of his earthly journey.

The next morning the priest told those around him about the dream and what Padre Pio had said to him about his approaching death. They did not attach much importance to all this. After all, it was only a dream! The priest thought otherwise and prepared for death with great care. One morning, fifteen days later, he was found dead in his bedroom.

CHAPTER 5

Worldwide "Travels"

Padre Pio had the gift of bilocation, that is, he could be present and active in two places at the same time. Although he had never been away from the monastery at San Giovanni Rotondo between 1916 and his death in 1968, his presence was noticed in different parts of the world, either in person or by a lingering perfume associated with him.

One day, in conversation with some of his confreres on this subject, he said, "The one to whom this happens knows what he wants, where he is going and why, but he does not know whether it is only his spirit that moves or whether he is present there body and soul." This remains a mystery of the Power of God. Here are a few episodes relating to this phenomenon.

Deathbed absolution in Turin

One day Padre Pio paused in front of a window in the corridor of the monastery at San Giovanni Rotondo. Suddenly he was caught up by some distant vision and rooted to the spot. A friar passing that way went up to him, greeted him, and kissed his hand, but Padre Pio was oblivious to all this. He was completely absorbed in his thoughts and pronouncing the words of absolution used in the confessional. When he came round again, he noticed some of the friars had gathered around him: "Ah! You are here! I did not notice. I was contemplating the mountain."

A few days later, the Superior of San Giovanni Rotondo received a telegram thanking him for having sent Padre Pio to Turin to give absolution to a sick man just at the moment of his death.

"Go ahead! I will follow you."

In September 1955, some people from the parish of Our Lady of Grace of San Severo, who were accompanied by some Capuchins, went on a pilgrimage to the shrine of Our Lady of Tears in Syracuse. The priests came to Padre Pio before setting out on their journey, to ask his prayers and blessing, but also to invite him to join them if he so wished. At this invitation Padre Pio said, "Go ahead! I will follow you." He did not, however, leave San Giovanni Rotondo.

The pilgrims started out, and when they came within the vicinity of Cosenza, they saw a huge field of melons and could not resist the urge to feast on them. They stopped the bus, bought some melons from the farmer, and gorged themselves! But melons are not easy to digest, and overheated by the sun, the melons produced quite disastrous effects on the pilgrims' gastrointestinal systems! The bus set out again but could not go far because the pilgrims had to scatter around the fields to get rid of the aftermath of this meal! Finally, they set out and reached Syracuse without any more stops! They visited the shrine, prayed for all their intentions, and took the bus home.

On the way, the driver had to stop because the road was blocked. He stepped out of the bus to have a look and then told the travelers that he could not drive through. Anxious, they all began to invoke Padre Pio to help them out of this situation. Immediately, as was normal when Padre Pio was around, there was a strong perfume that seemed to come in waves. Then the pilgrims saw some policemen making their rounds and unblocking the road, and so the journey continued without incident.

On their return, the pilgrims went to find Padre Pio who had just finished saying Mass and was preparing to make his thanksgiving. He looked at them in a good-natured way, and with a slightly mocking smile, said, "That was a fine show you made with those melons! And that was quite a scare on the Palermo road the other night!"

Incidents relating to the Marchioness Rizzani Boschi

The Marchioness Giovanna Rizzani Boschi told me about her experiences of Padre Pio's power of bilocation. These took place at Udine, in Rome, at San Giovanni Rotondo, in Naples, and again at San Giovanni Rotondo.

Padre Pio at Udine

During a visit I made to her when she was settled in Rome, the Marchioness told me of the circumstances surrounding her birth in Udine. These same circumstances were recorded in a written account by Padre Pio himself.

He writes: "Some days ago (this was in February 1905 when Padre Pio was a Capuchin student at the monastery in Sant'Elia a Pianisi), a very unusual thing happened to me, a kind of adventure. One night, about eleven o'clock on January 28 of this year, I was in the choir with Brother Anastasio. Suddenly, I found myself far from there, in a grand house where the father was dying just as his daughter was being born. The Virgin Mary appeared to me and said, 'I entrust this little one to you. This is a rough diamond. Work on her, polish her, and make her shine as brilliantly as possible because I will adorn myself with her.' I asked, 'But how can I do this? I am just a poor clerical student and don't even know if I will ever be a priest, and even if I do become a priest, how can I take care of her from so far away?' The Blessed Virgin replied, 'Don't worry! She will come to you, but you will meet her for the first time at St. Peter's in Rome!'"

This document was carefully preserved with Padre Pio's personal effects at San Giovanni Rotondo, but the Marchioness Giovanna grew up without knowing of its existence and without knowing who Padre Pio was. A long time later, when she had become a faithful follower of Padre Pio and privileged to collaborate with him, she came to know about the document and asked Padre Pio about it. He confirmed the authenticity of the facts it related.

In the aisles of St. Peter's, Rome

One summer afternoon in 1922, a university student, still known as Giovanna Boschi, was walking through St. Peter's in Rome with a friend. She was looking for some knowledgeable priest to talk to so that she might clear up some doubts she had about her faith.

After looking here and there without finding anyone, she noticed a sacristan and asked if there was a priest to whom she could talk. The good man told her that it was nearly time to close the building. "Why don't you look around," he said, "and maybe you'll find a priest who has been delayed. There is still half an hour left."

Giovanna went back and forth in the area and finally noticed a young Capuchin in a confessional. She went in and told him of her doubts and was given helpful answers. Then she went off to find her friend. She told her friend how happy she felt and asked her to wait until the Capuchin left the confessional so that she could kiss his hand. She had a good wait! The Capuchin did not come out. She went to see, but the confessional was empty. She inquired of the sacristan about where the priest might have gone, but he told her he had not seen any friar. Giovanna was surprised because she knew she had seen him and spoken to him.

"Giovanna! I know you!"

The following year, she went for her very first visit to San Giovanni Rotondo, as companion to an aunt who wanted to go to Padre Pio for confession. They were shown into the corridor between the old church and the monastery. She was told the priest would pass by, and she sat in the front row.

When Padre Pio arrived, he noticed her right away and said, "Giovanna! I know you! You were born on the day your father died." Giovanna, startled by this revelation, wondered how he knew of the circumstances of her birth. The next day she went to confession and Padre Pio told her, "My daughter, at last you have come! I have waited so many years for you!"

"Father," the young girl replied, "what do you want from me? I do not know you, and this is the first time I have been to San Giovanni Rotondo. I came with my aunt. You must be confusing me with some other girl."

"No," Padre Pio said, "I am not confusing you with anyone else. You already know me."

She insisted, "No, Father, I assure you, I do not know you."

Padre Pio continued, "Last summer, one afternoon, you went with a friend to St. Peter's in Rome to find a priest who could throw some light on your doubts of faith. Am I right?"

"Yes, Father," Giovanna replied, "you are right."

He told her of the Capuchin who had listened to her, resolved her doubts, and restored her peace of soul. She remembered it well. "I was that Capuchin!" Padre Pio said and then went on to tell her of the events surrounding her birth at Udine connected with the death of her father. Giovanna was deeply moved by these revelations and asked Padre Pio what she should do. He mapped out her mission in these words: "Come often to San Giovanni Rotondo, and I will take care of your soul, and you will learn God's will for you." From that day on the Marchioness Boschi became Padre Pio's faithful and privileged collaborator.

A slap in the face from Padre Pio!

Although, to a certain extent, I was personally involved in this story, I would not have known the sequence of events had not Marchioness Boschi told me herself. Many years ago she lived in Naples on Via del Casale near the Via Marechiaro where I lived.

I came to know her because my community had asked her husband, an engineer, to undertake some work on our house. This meant that, on occasion, I had to call at the home of Marchioness Boschi. In the course of a conversation we spoke of Padre Pio, whom I had known since 1940. From time to time she came to our community chapel for confession and Holy Communion. One day she arrived at about nine in the morning, and I went down to hear her confession and give her Communion and then went back to my room.

Later, in Rome, she asked me if, on that morning she went to confession, I had heard the sound of a slap or had looked outside the confessional.

During our conversation the Marchioness said to me quite suddenly, "Do you know that the day I went to you for confession, Padre Pio gave me a slap?"

"A slap!" I said. "But I heard nothing!"

"Maybe you didn't," she replied, "but I did, and how!" She then went on to explain that Padre Pio, seeing that she had developed the habit of confessing sins already mentioned in previous confessions, forbade her to do this. She kept on doing this, however, until one day he said to her, "Next time you do that, I will give you a slap!"

On that morning he had kept his word!

Farewell to Padre Pio

During the last two weeks of September 1968, I was passing through San Giovanni Rotondo. As a rule I always went to visit Padre Pio at the monastery. When I learned that he was quite ill, I did not want to disturb him and made up my mind I would see him when he was feeling better.

On my return to Naples, several days later, I heard on the radio that Padre Pio had died. I was deeply grieved and in great sorrow and did not want to believe that he was gone. It seemed to me that Padre Pio should never die!

I wanted to know all the details about his death, but the press only gave brief accounts. I was to learn all about his death later, during a visit to the Marchioness in Rome. She told me that she had to be away from San Giovanni Rotondo during the final months of Padre Pio's life. One day she heard a voice say to her, "Come immediately to San Giovanni because I am going. If you delay, you will never see me again!" She set out immediately with her friend Marguerite Hamilton, and they both stayed in a small hotel near the monastery.

A few days before his death, Padre Pio said to the Marchioness, "This is the last confession you will make to me. I absolve you from every sin you have committed from the age of reason until now."

"Why, Father?" she asked.

"I have already told you," Padre Pio replied. "I will no longer be able to hear your confession because I am going away, and Jesus is coming to meet me."

Giovanna understood that Padre Pio was leaving this world. She came out of the confessional very moved and kissed his hand. She offered him 50,000 lire for the hospital Casa Sollievo della Sofferenza, but Padre Pio refused it, saying that soon she would need her money.

Although she assured him that she had enough money for her meal and her return journey to Rome, he repeated that she would need it soon. The Marchioness went back to the hotel room she shared with her friend.

At nightfall, after blessing the crowd that had come to San Giovanni for the International Congress of Prayer Groups, Padre Pio went to his cell. This blessing was to be his farewell to the world.

During the night of September 23, 1968, around 2:25 AM, Madame Boschi suddenly woke up crying that Padre Pio was dying! Her friend, Marguerite, thought the Marchioness was having a nightmare and tried to calm her, but to no avail. Quite sure of the death of Padre Pio, the Marchioness wanted to rush to the monastery. Marguerite had to dress quickly and go with her. They arrived just as one of the Capuchins announced the sad news to the crowd gathered in front of the church.

A few days later, the Marchioness told Father Alberto D'Apolito, who doubted her assertions, that she was present when Padre Pio died. She gave him such a precise and detailed account of all that had happened that the priest was convinced she had been present, in spirit, at the dramatic last moments of this holy man. She also gave me all the details.

In General Cadorna's tent

After the disastrous defeat at Caporetto in 1917, General Luigi Cadorna fell into a deep depression and decided to commit suicide.

One night, near Treviso, before retiring to his tent, he told the guard that on no account should anyone disturb him. Then, collapsing onto a chair, he took a pistol from his bedside table and loaded it. Just as he was pointing it to his head, he saw a Capuchin standing before him. The priest shook his finger at him, saying, "Come now, General, surely you are not going to do anything so stupid!" The officer was so over-whelmed by this happening that he forgot all about his idea of suicide. He did not know who this religious was or how he had come into his tent.

When the Capuchin had gone, the General stormed out and demanded why the guard had let the priest into his tent, contrary to his orders. The soldier, as surprised as his superior, replied that no one had gone past him. More mystified than ever, the general went back to his tent determined to get to the bottom of this incident.

Some years later, when the war was over, the press began to write about a certain Padre Pio, a religious with the stigmata and miraculous powers, who lived on the Gargano.

Consumed with curiosity, the General wanted to know more. One day, incognito, he went to San Giovanni Rotondo. At the monastery he asked to see Padre Pio and was told that if he waited in the corridor that led from the monastery to the sacristy, he would have a chance of seeing him. A few minutes later Padre Pio came along with some of his confreres. When he came to where the general was standing, he called out, "Hello, General! We escaped by the skin of our teeth that night didn't we?" The startled general recognized in Padre Pio's face and voice the Capuchin who had visited him in his tent on a certain night in 1917.

Meeting with Mother Speranza at the Holy Office in Rome

Mother Speranza, foundress of the Ancelle dell'Amore Misericordioso (Servants of Merciful Love), claimed that Padre Pio came to her every day at the Holy Office in Rome for an entire year. This is such an extraordinary story that one is inclined to dismiss it as fantasy if one did not believe in the Almighty Power of God and the testimony of a woman as saintly as Mother Speranza. She told this to Father Alberto D'Apolito in the course of an interview in February 1970.

"Mother," he said to her, "I am a Capuchin from San Giovanni Rotondo. I want to ask your prayers for myself and for the glorification of Padre Pio."

Mother Speranza, who was small and bent, raised her eyes and looked at him, saying, "I have always prayed for Padre Pio."

"Did you know him?" the priest asked.

"Yes, I saw him often."

"Where? At San Giovanni Rotondo?"

"No, I never went there."

"Then, where did you know him?"

"In Rome!"

"But Mother," the priest said, "Padre Pio only went to Rome once, when he was very young, on May 17, 1917, to accompany his sister who was entering an enclosed order at St. Bridget's convent. You were in Spain at that time. You must be mistaken and confusing Padre Pio with some other Capuchin."

"No," she replied, "I am not mistaken, it really was Padre Pio."

"Where in Rome did you see him?"

"I saw him every day, for a year, at the Holy Office. He wore mittens to cover his wounds. I greeted him, kissed his hand, and he spoke with me."

"In what year did you have these daily visits?"

"When I was working at the Holy Office between 1937 and 1939."

"Mother," Father D'Apolito said, "your story seems very strange and highly improbable. I can hardly believe it."

"Father, I have to tell you that I have never been subject to hallucinations, and I would add this to what I have said. A mysterious person used to fly in from Milan. He had a white beard, was very ugly, and I was afraid of him."

"Who was he?" the priest asked. "A friar?"

"I don't know. Whenever I saw him, I was struck with terror and wanted to run away. I had the impression he was some kind of demon!"

"What was his business at the Holy Office?"

"He came to testify against Padre Pio!"

"Mother, please do not be offended if I tell you that I find your story difficult to believe."

Without the slightest sign of resentment, Mother Speranza said quietly to Father D'Apolito, "Father, you can think what you want. I tell you again, I saw Padre Pio, in Rome, every day for a year. I have always prayed for him, and now I will pray for his beatification."

"Get rid of that friar!"

In June 1973 a woman came from Rome to San Giovanni Rotondo to give thanks to Padre Pio for the help he had given her dying husband. She told me what actually happened.

It was discovered that her husband had a malignant tumor. In the hospital he went through every conceivable treatment, but without any great hope of a cure. Back at home the sick man became aware of the incurable nature of his illness. He got worse day by day. His family had a great devotion to Padre Pio and so began praying to him to come to their assistance.

One day in his room the patient began to cry out in a loud voice, "Get rid of that friar! He tells me to go with him. Chase him away! I do not want to go!"

Those around his bed tried to calm him by telling him there was no friar to be seen.

"Why, can't you see him?" the sick man asked. "He is at the foot of my bed."

They told him again that no one was there and that he should calm down, which he eventually did. They asked him what the friar looked like. The man replied, "He was a Capuchin with a white beard, and he told me he would come back for me on February 5."

They showed him a photo of Padre Pio, and he recognized the friar immediately. "Yes, that's him!"

The family intensified their prayers, and the sick man appeared to be a little better. He was able to get up and go to church for Mass and Holy Communion, and he prayed fervently every day. Suddenly, on February 5, 1973, his health worsened, and he died peacefully in great serenity.

Padre Pio had kept his promise: He came for the man and brought him home to the Lord in the next life.

"Get away from here!"

This next incident happened on a battlefield during World War I. A captain was urging his soldiers to resist enemy attack. At a particular moment, he saw a friar with a pale face and sparkling eyes, who called out to him, "Get away from here, captain. Come to me! Quick! Quick!" Attracted by the face and the voice, the captain jumped up and went toward the friar. The captain had barely reached the priest when he heard the terrible explosion of a bomb that had dropped just where he had been standing!

Terror-stricken, the captain looked in that direction for a moment; then he turned around to thank the priest who had saved him. To his amazement, the priest was gone. The friar's face, nonetheless, was engraved on the officer's memory.

One day, when he was telling this story to friends, one of them suggested that perhaps the stigmatist at Gargano, Padre Pio, might be the person he saw that day. So the captain set out for San Giovanni Rotondo. Padre Pio had just finished Mass and was putting away the vestments in the sacristy. The captain looked closely at him and cried out, "That's the friar! That is certainly the friar I saw!" He went forward and threw himself at Padre Pio's feet, kissed his hand, and, overcome, thanked him.

The priest put his hand on the officer's head and said, "It's not me you should be thanking but Our Lord and the Blessed Virgin."

"I replied that night at the inn."

A young married couple from England had serious problems that caused them great distress. In an effort to help, one of their friends spoke to them of Padre Pio, about his stigmata, and how countless people came to him in their distress. The couple wrote to him to tell him of their situation.

Their letter was not answered. Although they were not financially well off, they decided to go in person to San Giovanni. On their journey they stopped at a cheap hotel in Bern, Switzerland. Their room was in a damp, moldy attic. It was winter and snowing. They became discouraged and wondered if it was worthwhile to continue on such an arduous and long journey with no guarantee that they would even meet Padre Pio at the end of it!

They were in this perplexed state of mind when, suddenly, a sweet perfume surrounded them and imparted a kind of comfort. They looked in every corner of the room to find out where it came from but could not find its source. The perfume disappeared just as suddenly as it had come. They asked the innkeeper about this phenomenon, but he was at great pains to assure them that no one had spread perfume in their room. The young couple remained intrigued by this incident.

When the couple arrived at San Giovanni, Padre Pio welcomed them as if he had always known them. They reminded him that they had written, and he had not replied. "What do you mean, I did not reply? I replied that night at the inn. Did you not smell the perfume?"

Then they realized that Padre Pio had come to their aid by encouraging them to keep going to San Giovanni Rotondo. He listened to them and helped them to solve their problems. The young couple returned to England, happy and at peace.

A guide in the desert

The newspaper, *Il Progresso Italo-Americano*, carried this story in its October 24, 1949, edition.

Pietro Cadice and his family lived in Rome. His son, Giacomo, was very unhappy at home, so ran he away and joined the French Foreign Legion. When his parents noticed his absence, they notified the police, who searched in vain for him. In time, the family of the young runaway received a letter saying he was at the Foreign Legion training camp in

Sidi-Bel-Abbès, Africa, that he had signed on for five years, and that he could not return home until his time was served. His father fell into a depression. He did not know what saint to turn to! A friend persuaded him to go to Padre Pio. Cadice told Padre Pio all that his son had done and begged Padre Pio to send him back home. After listening attentively, Padre Pio put his hand on Pietro's head and said, "Go and pray! By the third moon your son will return home!"

The following part of the story was told by the son when he returned home on the very date indicated by Padre Pio. The young man explained that one night, when, in a state of fever, he was on guard duty at an advanced post, he saw a friar who took him by the hand, inviting the soldier to follow him.

They went across the desert for several days and finally reached the coast. When they boarded a ship, the friar disappeared. The young man disembarked at Marseille, then went on to Sardinia, and he finally reached Rome and his family. It is not difficult to imagine everyone's joy at his return!

One puzzle remained, however. Who was the friar who had led the boy through the desert? Pietro showed his son a photo of Padre Pio. With tears in his eyes, the young man immediately recognized the priest as the one who had saved him. Padre Pio had kept his promise.

Padre Pio in California

The American newspaper *L'Italia e la Voce del Popolo*, edited in San Francisco, California, carried the following story on March 3, 1956, by Father G. Giuseppe Tursi, R.C.J., which tells of Padre Pio's presence in the city of Fresno, California, where he cured a sick man.

Bartolomeo Pollina, a Sicilian emigrant, lived for many years in the town of Fresno. He suffered from an incapacitating hernia that became dangerous. The doctors advised him to have an operation as soon as possible, but the sick man would not hear of the surgeon's knife!

Through reading he had come to know Padre Pio and the marvels he performed. He hoped that Padre Pio would cure him of his illness before he had to go into surgery. Bartolomeo wrote to the priest, asking him to intercede with the Lord on his behalf. In the reply Bartolomeo received he was told that Padre Pio was interested in his case, would pray for him, and that he should also pray and trust in the Lord.

Time went by and nothing happened. One night, however, just as he was about to retire to bed, Bartolomeo heard someone breathing heavily at the foot of his bed. He was afraid for a moment, but the rest of the night passed without incident. The next night the same thing happened, but this time the breathing came from the side of the bed. The third night he heard the breathing again, at the head of the bed. On the morning after the third day, Bartolomeo felt two hands working around the area of the hernia to put everything back in its natural position. He was wide awake and followed this "operation" trembling a little but fully convinced that Padre Pio had come to cure him. He then felt great interior peace. When he got up, he felt the affected area and realized he had, in fact, been cured. He was able to take up his full activities again without any fear of hurting himself.

Full of gratitude he wrote to Padre Pio to thank him for this cure and for having heard his prayers. He promised to live a more Christian life. In his reply, Padre Pio told Bartolomeo to thank the Lord and to trust him always.

"I know it better than you!"

In 1949 a church dedicated to the Holy Family was built in Pietrelcina (Benevento), Padre Pio's birthplace. When the work was finished, plans were made for the official opening to take place on May 20.

On the eve of this event Bishop Agostino Mancinelli was scheduled to consecrate the church. The Capuchin Superiors were trying to find a way to have Padre Pio present without creating a commotion among the people. They agreed to keep their idea an absolute secret! In spite of their efforts, word got out that Padre Pio was coming! The plan failed, and Padre Pio could not go to Pietrelcina. He did not seem to know anything about the opening of the new church.

Later, during a conversation, Father Alberto D'Apolito said to Padre Pio, "Spiritual Father (a name given to Padre Pio by his confreres), why don't you come some day and see the church? It is very beautiful."

Padre Pio replied, "I know it better than you!"

"Did you see a photograph of it, perhaps?" Father Alberto asked.

"No!" answered Padre Pio. "I went there. I can describe it in great detail. Do you know how many steps there are at the entrance?"

Father Alberto had never counted them.

The presence of Padre Pio at Pietrelcina was confirmed in the diary of the Provincial at the time, Father Agostino da San Marco in Lamis. One day he said to Padre Pio that he would be absolutely delighted to see a monastery open at Pietrelcina. Padre Pio said to him, "And you will be the Guardian (Superior), when you have finished serving as Provincial."

"Will you come to the ceremony?" Father Agostino asked.

"Yes," said Padre Pio. "I will be present and at the same time I will be here in San Giovanni Rotondo hearing confessions!"

Padre Pio in Uruguay

Msgr. Damiani, Vicar General of the Diocese of Salto in Uruguay, wanted to end his days in San Giovanni Rotondo, to be near Padre Pio. He spoke about his desire to Padre Pio, but the priest told him that his place was in the Diocese of Salto and not in San Giovanni Rotondo. Msgr. Damiani then asked Padre Pio to come and help him at the moment of death. After praying for a moment, Padre Pio agreed to do this.

This is how this promise was kept according to the account of events given by Archbishop Barbieri of Montevideo.

In 1941 Msgr. Alfredo Viola, Archbishop of Salto, was celebrating his priestly jubilee with several other bishops, among them, Archbishop Barbieri. During sleep Msgr. Viola heard someone knock on his bedroom door. Suddenly he was wide awake. A Capuchin came into his room and said to him, "Go to Msgr. Damiani. He is dying." Msgr. Barbieri got up right away, put on some clothes, took the holy oils, and with some other priests went to Msgr. Damiani's bedside. He was, in fact, dying, but he was very lucid. After receiving the sacrament of the Sick he died very peacefully.

On the bedside table Msgr. Barbieri found a piece of paper on which the following words were written in a very shaky hand: "Padre Pio came!" He decided to keep this note so that he could check out the facts on his next trip to Italy.

On April 13, 1949, taking advantage of the *Ad Limina* visit every bishop makes to the Pope from time to time, he decided to visit Padre Pio. When they met he immediately recognized the Capuchin who had come to his room that night. However, to make quite sure, he questioned Padre Pio about his visit to Uruguay. Padre Pio remained silent, preferring to say nothing. Msgr. Barbieri, afraid that he had perhaps not understood what he was asking, repeated the question but Padre Pio still remained silent.

Msgr. Barbieri realized that the event had really happened, so he said to Padre Pio: "I understand." Padre Pio said to him, "But, of course, you understand!"

"We cannot find Padre Pio!"

A luxury car drew up one day in the square at the monastery of San Giovanni Rotondo. Several grand ladies got out accompanied by a conceited young man who made it quite clear he had come to ridicule Padre Pio. He asked some people nearby where he could find Padre Pio. They told him he would be in the sacristy where he heard confessions. The young man disappeared into the church and went to the sacristy. "Where is Padre Pio?" he demanded to know. He was told that the priest had just left to go to the church. He must surely have passed him? "No! I didn't see him," said the young man. "But that's impossible!" he was told. "Padre Pio went out the door you just came through!"

The young man and his party were becoming rather annoyed. They asked some Capuchins who were nearby to find Padre Pio. They searched everywhere, but in vain. Padre Pio was nowhere to be found!

After a fruitless search the Capuchins apologized to the group, declaring that they were puzzled by Padre Pio's absence.

The young man was really annoyed and said, "He must have gone out! Where is he likely to have gone?" The priests told him, "Padre Pio never leaves the monastery! We have no idea where he might be!"

More furious than ever, and feeling extremely let down and frustrated, the young man and the ladies went back to their car, fuming, and drove away. Those standing around saw the car disappear. But what did they see when they turned round? Padre Pio was standing there! They told him how they had searched everywhere for him without success. "I was here all the time," he told them. "I walked back and forth in front of you, but you did not see me!" Then he went into the church to hear confessions.

A thwarted air raid

During World War II a general at the American base near Bari heard that the Germans had an arms depot somewhere around San Giovanni Rotondo. He planned an air raid to destroy the depot, and he led the squadron on this mission. Nearing the target, he saw a friar ascend into the air with his arms outstretched! Suddenly the controls on the planes no longer responded. So they dropped their bombs in the forest, turned around, and went back to base.

The general could not understand. He talked about the incident to the officers and pilots, but no one could come up with a reasonable explanation. Who was this friar who had obstructed their mission and disabled the planes' communication system? What a mystery!

One day, the general overheard someone speaking of Padre Pio, who lived on Mount Gargano and worked miracles.

Suspecting that this was the friar who had thwarted the bombardment, he went to San Giovanni Rotondo to see him.

The priest came toward him, put his hand on his shoulder, and said, "Ah! So you are the one who wanted to kill us all!" The astounded general was won over by the eyes and personality of Padre Pio. He became a Catholic and a friend and follower of Padre Pio until the end of his days.

It is worth noting an additional and curious detail: When Padre Pio spoke to the general, he used the Benevento dialect, yet the American heard every word in perfect English!

Padre Pio at Maglie (Lecce)

The father of one of the Capuchins at the Maglie (Lecce) monastery was seriously ill, the victim of a spinal cord disease. He was unable to walk and finally became bedridden. It was said he would never walk again. His son, who knew Padre Pio and had great confidence in him, wrote him to ask his urgent intercession with the Lord for his father who was slowly dying. Padre Pio wrote back, assuring the Capuchin that he was praying for his father and urging him to trust in God.

The days went on, and the illness took its relentless course. One afternoon, the sick man suddenly saw a bearded friar near his bed who spoke to him, "You are suffering! Suffer with patience!" The same thing happened the next day and the day after, and for seven days more, but the sick man's condition did not change. On the contrary, it became worse! On the tenth day it was thought that he should receive the sacrament of the Sick. That afternoon the same friar reappeared, saying, "Look here now! That's enough!"

From that moment the illness subsided, and the sick man felt much better. Eventually he was completely cured. He was able to take up his life again and go back to his work in the fields.

His son understood that Padre Pio had been part of God's providential plan in all this, and he wrote to thank him.

The blaspheming potter

An old proverb says, "Better to light a candle than curse the dark!" Curses had been plentiful for some time around a potter from Torre Maggiore because he could not get his furnace started due to the sirocco. He was hopping mad! He was losing money and his living because he could not fire his pottery. He had almost exhausted his litany of swear words, curses, and blasphemies when he thought he would add Padre Pio's name to the list! Suddenly a friar came up behind him and said, "Peace be with you!" Peace was the last thing on his mind! He told the friar that he would have no peace as long as the cursed wind kept him from using his furnace. Padre Pio repeated, "Peace be with you!"

The friar sat down on a crate and with a gesture asked for some fire. Seeing the potter beside himself with rage, the priest added, "I will light it myself!"

The potter retorted, "Perhaps you are like that Padre Pio who works miracles for simpletons?"

The priest replied, "I am Padre Pio!"

The fire lit immediately, and the potter just had time to hear the friar say before he disappeared, "Don't be afraid, Michael, and stop swearing!"

Orders from a loudspeaker

During the turmoil that followed the collapse of fascism in Italy, a young woman who was a follower of Padre Pio was unjustly denounced as a "collaborator." She was arrested by partisans and condemned to death after a summary trial. Although she was completely innocent, she had no way of proving this. In great distress during this terrible trial she invoked Padre Pio in her heart, asking him to come to her assistance.

Meanwhile, she was taken down the road to the place of execution. Suddenly, just as the execution squad was about to cross the road, a column of tanks, ambulances, and troops passed through, coming from the south en route to the north. The partisans had to wait until this convoy passed through, and the young woman knew that when the last vehicle passed, she would be on her way again to be shot.

She called all the more on Padre Pio's help. The military vehicles took much longer than expected to go past, and some of the partisans grew tired of waiting. So they began leaving, until only their leader remained doggedly at his post.

In the meantime some friends of the young girl heard of her predicament and set about getting evidence to prove her innocence to the authorities concerned.

Just as she started out again on the road to her death, a car drew up alongside, and a man leaned out saying she had been freed and offered her a lift home!

When she got home she found hooligans were looting and vandalizing her house. They thought she had been killed and were helping themselves to her possessions. Her terrified sister could do nothing but watch. Suddenly, a very loud voice, like a loudspeaker, cried out twice: "That's enough! That's enough!" At this, the looters left everything and ran.

The young woman attributed this and her liberation to Padre Pio's intervention. As soon as she could, she went to San Giovanni Rotondo to thank Padre Pio. The priest welcomed her and, smiling, said, "What confidence you have, my daughter! If you only knew how you had me running for you!"

A strange way to get out

When news of Padre Pio's stigmata got out, people flocked to him out of curiosity or for confession. This influx of people grew daily and meant a great deal of apostolic work not only for Padre Pio but for the other friars as well. The church was too small to hold such crowds, especially in the summer when there was a great danger of people being crushed.

One day in summer, the church was so packed that the atmosphere was suffocating. Some people in the crowd were near to passing out. The entrance was blocked by the crowds. Padre Pio decided to leave the confessional to go outside. He did this in a rather unusual way! Without anyone seeing him, he went through the throng by an odd route. Everyone saw that he was no longer in the confessional, but no one had seen him leave.

Father Agostino, who was Padre Pio's former Provincial and spiritual director, asked him how he had moved through a crowd that was packed together like sardines.

"I walked on their shoulders!" Padre Pio replied.

"And what about their heads?" Father Agostino asked. "Did they not get in the way?"

"No Father, they were like pebbles under my feet!"

A pervading perfume

Giuseppe Onofrio worked in the Tax Department. In 1942 he was at the office in Rieti and then transferred to Lucera in the Province of Foggia. He had been an atheist since his youth and had only gone to church to get married. On this occasion he went to confession, made his First Communion, and then received the sacrament of Confirmation. After that he led a peaceful Christian life.

At Lucera he heard people speak of Padre Pio and the wonderful things he did. Onofrio wanted to meet this friar. In April 1943 an opportunity came up, and he went to the little Capuchin church at San Giovanni Rotondo.

When he saw Padre Pio and attended his Mass, something stirred within Onofrio. He wanted to go to confession. When he came face to face with the priest, he was asked a question he could not answer. Padre Pio told him to go to the church and wait there until he was called. He had to wait a long time. He began to lose patience. He was about to leave when he was called, and the confession began, through-out which Padre Pio held Onofrio's right hand. The confession ended, and Onofrio left, but he noticed a perfume coming from the hand Padre Pio had held. This scent lasted for two months.

He had occasion to visit Padre Pio again. This time he asked the priest's advice on whether or not he should ask for a transfer. Padre Pio said he could, but he would encounter many difficulties. Onofrio, nevertheless, asked for a change, and he had to move often. He noticed, however, that through all these moves, the aroma of Padre Pio's perfume remained on his right hand. He finally got the post he wanted and settled in Palermo.

On December 18, 1944, he came again to see Padre Pio, this time with all his family. They came to thank the priest and to go to confession. The first to go into the confessional was Onofrio's little daughter. Without ever having seen her before, Padre Pio said, "Your dad is happy now, isn't he?" Then it was her little brother's turn. Padre Pio had never met him either. He asked, "What are you doing here? You are already in a state of grace. Go, and remain that way forever!"

Behind the bishop

Bishop D'Indico, from Florence, had a sister who had contracted paratyphoid A and B and was in a coma. Her condition was desperate. Her parents had written to Padre Pio asking his intercession so that their daughter might be cured. On July 20, 1921, Bishop D'Indico was alone in his office when he had the feeling that someone was standing behind him. He turned around just in time to see a friar walking away. He thought of Padre Pio and was afraid.

Bishop D'Indico quickly left his office. While walking, he met one of his chaplains and told him what had happened. The priest did not believe the story and thought the bishop was suffering from hallucinations brought on by the stress of his sister's impending death. To take the bishop's mind off things, the priest invited him to go for a walk.

On their return to the bishop's house, they were called by the sick woman who had suddenly come out of the coma. She told them that Padre Pio had come to her and had said, "Do not be afraid! Tomorrow your fever will disappear, and in a few days there will be no trace of the illness in your body." She told him she thought he was a saint who had come to heal her.

She commended her husband and daughter to his prayers, then asked permission to kiss his hand. Padre Pio held out his hands, with the stigmata, and taking his leave said, "I leave you with the memory of my visit of July 20, 1921."

In a few days the woman was completely recovered, as Padre Pio had predicted.

Other cases of Padre Pio's power of bilocation

In July 1921, Padre Pio went to the bedside of the dying Bishop Paolo Schinosi of Benevento, who had ordained him a priest on August 10, 1910.

Cleonice Morcaldi relates that one day Padre Pio visited her sister in a convent in Rome, through bilocation and, in the same way, went to America on Christmas night to see her father, Grazio Forgione:

> Colonel Russo of Caserta tells that during World War II, he was a prisoner of war in a camp in India. Padre Pio came to visit the prisoners every night. When the war was over, many of these men, on coming home, went to San Giovanni Rotondo to thank the priest. Padre Pio knew each and everyone of them.
>
> Don Orione, considered to be a saint, says that he saw Padre Pio in St. Peter's, in Rome, at the time of the canonization of St. Teresa of the Child Jesus.
>
> Gaetano Pavone, an engineer, was a gunner in the U.S. Air Force. While flying over Mount Gargano, between the lakes of Verano and Lesina, he saw Padre Pio appear before him covering the whole sky! For a long time, Pavone did not want to talk about this fearing he would be laughed at, but he told his wife on September 23, 1968, the day Padre Pio died. As might be expected, she dismissed this story.

It is also recorded that Padre Pio went to Budapest and brought Cardinal Mindszenty everything he needed to celebrate Mass when he took refuge in the American embassy.

It is also known that Padre Pio celebrated Mass for Sisters in a convent in Czechoslovakia. The Sisters were so convinced of the reality of his presence that, after Mass, they went to thank him and offer him a cup of coffee. Imagine their surprise when they could not find the priest who had, meanwhile, disappeared!

All these accounts of bilocation are certainly not the only times Padre Pio used this power. He was very careful not to divulge the gifts given him by God. Reported here are only those stories and circumstances of which we have learned and heard.

CHAPTER 6

The Path to Health

Many came to Padre Pio in his lifetime, and still more do today, to ask him to intercede with God for better health.

He was very careful to point out, and sometimes with characteristic vigor, that it was the Lord who was responsible for the cures effected and not he. His role was simply to pray for those in suffering. The fact remains, however, that when Padre Pio prayed, the Lord cured.

The list of healings would be too long to include here. We have limited ourselves to the most striking cures in order to show clearly that for many unfortunate people, Padre Pio was their path to health according to the plan of God.

At a particular moment, Padre Pio wondered, "The Lord grants spectacular cures to many people, but what of those who are not part of this divine plan? Have they to bear this cross of ill health? Can't something be done for them too?"

This gave Padre Pio the idea to take on the huge task of building the Casa Sollievo della Sofferenza (the House for the

Relief of Suffering). In his mind, this was not simply to be a hospital but a house, a safe haven for his brothers, bearing the image of Christ, who would be cared for as if they were Christ himself. Jesus had, in fact, said, "Whatever you do to the least of my brothers, you do unto me."

This "house" was to be a model in all aspects: human, Christian, medical, scientific, and technical. To launch this great enterprise, Padre Pio called on everyone to help, and offerings came from all over the world. It is interesting, however, to know how the first "financial stone" was laid.

When news got out that Padre Pio was building the Casa, a little old woman came up to him and offered a small gold coin. Padre Pio saw how poor this woman was and said to her, "Thank you! But you should keep this for yourself. You need it!"

"No, Father," she replied, "take it!"

He insisted that she keep it: "You can't take the bread out of your mouth! Do as I say, and keep it for your own needs."

The woman had a qualm about this and felt mortified. "You are right, Father," she said. "This is too small!" Padre Pio was very moved by this and said to her, "Please, give it to me and may God bless you!"

When the time came to consider the financing of the Casa's construction, Padre Pio said to the management committee, "I will start it off!" He gave them the little gold coin.

There is certainly an echo of the Gospel here!

The dead baby in the suitcase

A six-month-old baby was in a state of bad health that brought him close to death. The poor mother, who had great faith, thought she might save the baby by taking him to Padre Pio so that he might intercede with God for a cure.

It was a long distance to travel but, full of courage, she took the train. During the journey, due either to the child's serious condition or the rigors of travel, the baby died. The desolate mother wrapped the body in some clothes and put it in a fiber suitcase.

On arrival at the church she ran up the steps and, suitcase in hand, took her place in the line of women waiting for confession. When her turn came, she threw herself at Padre Pio's feet and, crying pitifully, opened the suitcase.

Dr. Sanguinetti, a convert and Padre Pio's right-hand man at the Casa Sollievo della Sofferenza, was present at this incident. He realized immediately that, even if the baby had not died of the illness, he most certainly would have died of suffocation, being closed in the suitcase for so long. At the sight of the dead infant Padre Pio paled and was gripped by emotion. He raised his eyes to heaven, prayed for a few moments, and then turned abruptly to the mother, saying, "Why are you crying so loud? Can't you see that your son is sleeping?"

It was true! The baby was now sleeping peacefully. The happiness of this mother was beyond description, as were her cries of great joy and those of everyone who witnessed what had happened.

Sight without pupils

Can a person see without pupils? It is not humanly possible. There is, however, someone still living today who was born without pupils and who now sees. From the moment Padre Pio made the Sign of the Cross on her eyes, she began to see, and even to this day she still has no pupils! Her name is Gemma di Giorgi. Born on Christmas night, 1939, her parents noticed she had strange eyes. Something was missing. The village doctor consulted two specialists in Palermo, Dr. Cucco and Dr. Contino. These men examined the little girl and discovered she had no pupils. Their prognosis was that she would be blind for the rest of her life because no one can see without pupils.

The parents were devastated by this news. They nevertheless trusted Divine Providence and often prayed in the Chapel of Our Lady at the church. One day they had a visit from an aunt, who was a nun. She advised them to contact Padre Pio. The little girl's grandmother was quite prepared to accompany her to San Giovanni Rotondo. She asked the nun to write to Padre Pio and commend the little blind girl to his prayers. One night the nun dreamed of the priest, and he asked her, "Where is this Gemma for whom you bombard me with prayers?" Still in the dream, the nun brought Gemma to him, and he made the Sign of the Cross on her eyes.

The next day she received a letter from Padre Pio. It read: "Dear daughter, I assure you of my prayers for the little one. Best wishes!" Impressed by the coincidence between the dream and Padre Pio's reply to her letter, she urged the little girl's grandmother to take her right away to San Giovanni Rotondo. The old lady had no need to be told twice, so she took her granddaughter and set out without delay. On the train Gemma told her grandmother that she thought she could see something, but the grandmother did not believe her because no one can see without pupils.

On arriving, Gemma and her grandmother went quickly to the church and to Padre Pio for confession. The little girl had not yet made her first Confession and Communion, and this seemed a good opportunity for her to receive these Sacraments from the hands of Padre Pio himself.

The grandmother told the little girl to ask Padre Pio, in the confessional, to pray that she might see, but Gemma forgot. When Gemma came to him, Padre Pio put his hands on her eyes and made the Sign of the Cross.

After confession the grandmother asked Gemma if she had thought to petition Padre Pio for her sight. The little girl told her she had forgotten to do so. The woman was very upset at this and began to cry. She then went off to find Padre Pio herself and intercede for Gemma's cure. Padre Pio said to her, "Have confidence, my daughter. You must not make Gemma cry, and you must not worry about her. Gemma sees, you know!"

The little girl received her First Holy Communion from Padre Pio, who after giving her the host again made the Sign of the Cross on her eyes. On the day set for their return journey, Gemma and her grandmother took the train home. The little girl noticed that her sight was getting better and better, to the point of being normal.

At Cosenza the grandmother became ill and had to stay in the hospital for a few days. Before leaving she took Gemma to an oculist who was absolutely astounded to discover that the girl could see perfectly well although she had no pupils!

A few months later Gemma went with her parents to a specialist in Perugia. He also attested to the fact that she could see normally even without pupils and admitted that there was no human explanation for this.

Gemma still sees like this. She lives in her village, but, from time to time, she leaves it to tell her wonderful story!

A rigid leg bends!

On June 26, 1946, Giuseppe Canaponi, a railwayman, was riding his motorcycle to work when a truck hit him. He was taken to the hospital with a broken left leg and other more critical injuries. His life was saved, but his leg remained rigid.

Canaponi could not accept this and did everything to recover the use of his leg. He went to many reputable orthopedic hospitals, but to no avail. He despaired of ever being well again. He was in full vigor and had a wife and son to support, yet he could only take a few steps with the help of two canes. In his most depressed moments he became angry and would insult everybody and swear. Then he would regret his behavior, calm himself, and get back to normal.

One day his wife spoke to him of Padre Pio and suggested that he go to see him. At first, Canaponi reacted violently and spoke against the priest. In the end he allowed himself to be persuaded and set out for San Giovanni Rotondo with his wife and child. At the church he asked for Padre Pio. As soon as the priest saw Canaponi, he said, "You curse and swear a lot, you insult everyone, and you get upset with yourself!"

Canaponi replied, "Yes, Father, I do."

"But afterward," the priest went on, "you are sorry and go to your room to pray."

Then Padre Pio began to list all the sins the man had committed in his life. Canaponi was quite astounded and asked the priest how he could know all this when they had only just met. He also asked Padre Pio, "Father, pray to the Lord for me that he might rid me of this terrible fault." Padre Pio replied, "You must be strong; otherwise it is useless for the Lord to give you his grace."

Without having noticed it, Canaponi was kneeling before Padre Pio, in spite of his rigid leg! On getting up he noticed that the stiffness had gone. He put his canes under his arm and went into the church where his wife and son were waiting. When his wife saw him walking normally, she could not believe her eyes, but their son convinced her because he had seen his father kneeling and getting up again.

Back at their hotel, Canaponi wanted to make sure his leg was really cured. He put a cushion on the floor and knelt down and got up again several times. Everything was normal again! The next day he went back to the church to thank Padre Pio. "I did not cure you," Padre Pio said. "Thank the Lord, and him alone, for this grace."

Back home Canaponi was submitted repeatedly to ortho-pedic tests. The wonderful thing is that x-rays showed that the leg was still rigid, yet he was enjoying complete mobility!

A doctor turns to God

Dr. Antonio Scarparo, who practiced medicine in Padua, discovered one day that he had cancer. There was no doubt about it. He, better than anyone, recognized the symptoms.

His brother Giovanni, who often went to see Padre Pio, told him about his brother's case and asked what could be done. Padre Pio advised an operation. The doctor had the operation in 1960 and everything seemed quite normal again. In May 1962, however, the illness reappeared. An x-ray taken by Dr. Bruno Bonomini revealed "a lung infection caused by testicular seminoma." He had three months to live!

When Padre Pio heard this, he said, "He must take care of himself." The sick man came to San Giovanni Rotondo and showed the x-rays to Padre Pio who blessed them. Dr. Scarparo begged him, "Obtain this one grace for me! I have three children!" Padre Pio replied, "That is so sad!"

The doctor went back to Padua while his brother remained in San Giovanni Rotondo to plead his cause with Padre Pio.

"Father," he said, "the doctors have given my brother only three months to live!"

Padre Pio replied, "Don't worry so much! That's what they say!"

Then the following dialogue took place between Padre Pio and Giovanni Scarparo:

"Father, you have said that to obtain this grace one must have faith. I am asking you for this faith."

"Faith comes through good works."

"Father, there are no drugs to help my brother, but just one thought from you and he will be cured."

"Yes, if God wants it."

"But it was Jesus who said, 'If you have faith the size of a mustard seed, you can say to this mountain: "Move!" and to this sycamore: "Be uprooted and go plant yourself in the sea."'"

"And do you have this faith?"

"No! I don't. But *you* do!"

"But if you do not have this faith, how can you ask this grace of the Lord?"

"I don't know if I have it, and even if I did have it, I don't know how much!"

"I understand! I understand! You have even less than a grain of mustard seed!"

While this conversation was taking place between Padre Pio and Giovanni Scarparo, Dr. Bonomini, in Padua, was studying the results of the x-rays, over and over again. He began to realize that there was no trace of cancer!

When Giovanni heard this, he went back to Padre Pio to tell him. The priest simply said, "Let us thank the Lord!" Scarparo added, "Father, I made a vow that if my brother was cured, I would give up smoking." "Well," said Padre Pio, "stop right now!" Dr. Antonio Scarparo was completely and definitively cured.

A cripple is healed

One day in 1919, a beggar, who was also crippled, came to the Capuchin monastery door at San Giovanni Rotondo. His name was Francesco Viscio, but he was nicknamed Santaredda. He was forty-three-years old. An illness contracted in the early months of his life had left him with his feet turned inward so badly that he needed crutches to walk. When he did not have these, he crawled about on all fours.

The children of San Giovanni Rotondo made fun of Viscio and laughed at him. They would take away his crutches so that he had to crawl on his hands and knees. All he could do to defend himself was to yell at them.

Every day he went to the monastery for something to eat, and there was always plenty even when the number of beggars had increased, as was the case on that day in 1919. On that particular day, Viscio was tired of such a life, and seeing Padre Pio go by called out to him, "Father, grant me a favor!" The priest stopped, looked at him intently, and said in dialect, "Throw away your crutches!" The unfortunate man did not quite understand and was hesitant. Again Padre Pio called even more loudly to him, "Throw away your crutches!" Torn between incredulity and hope, the beggar tried to get up, and succeeded! He did it again and realized that he was able to walk normally.

The man was overcome with joy and astonishment as was everyone around who witnessed the incident. This was the beginning of a new life for Viscio. Several years later, Viscio died.

Antonio Egidio, one of Padre Pio's spiritual sons, on recalling this case, asked the priest, "When a cripple like Santaredda goes to heaven, tell me, what happens to him?" Padre Pio remained silent and pensive for a moment, then, with a start, he pointed to the ceiling and said, "Look! This is what happens!" Egidio looked up and saw an opening in the sky that revealed Viscio in paradise, resplendent in glory. This vision lasted but an instant and then vanished. When Egidio turned to Padre Pio, the friar also had disappeared!

God's plans take time

Padre Pio told Mr. and Mrs. Pennisi that God had a plan for the cure of their sick daughter Maria, but they did not have the patience to follow the plan step by step. Their daughter was cured, all the same, but she suffered the consequences of her parents' impatience.

The girl was born in New York but returned to Italy with her parents. They settled in Pietrelcina, the home village of Padre Pio. Soon afterward, in 1922, Maria contracted tuberculosis—at that time the disease was relentless. She coughed continually and suffered pain in her right shoulder.

The parents did everything in their power for their child's cure, but to no avail. They took her to Naples for tests by excellent doctors, among them the saintly Joseph Moscati. After examining her thoroughly, he had to agree with his colleagues that the little girl had an incurable type of TB and would die soon. Her parents brought her back to Pietrelcina and did everything they could to alleviate her suffering.

One day, Maria's father decided to take her to Padre Pio. Because his wife could not come with him that day, he went with a sister-in-law. Padre Pio had never heard of the sick girl, nor had he ever met her, yet he said to her, "You are Maria Pennesi, are you sick? No, you are in better health than I am!" And he put his hand on her shoulder. At this point the father thought it his duty to let the priest know that his daughter was seriously ill and that he had brought her to him for a cure. Padre Pio replied, "Don't worry! I will take care of her!"

They went back to the hotel, and the next day the girl said she felt better and wanted to go to the church at the monastery to receive Holy Communion from Padre Pio. She did this for eight consecutive days. The father then decided it was time to go back to Pietrelcina because his daughter had to go to school. Nonetheless, before leaving he went to ask Padre Pio's advice on the matter. Padre Pio advised him, "She should go back to school but only after the Christmas break."

"But, Father," the man said, "you can cure her just as easily from a distance."

"No!" said Padre Pio, "you must leave her here at San Giovanni. I want to keep an eye on her!"

Mr. Pennesi did not want to take this advice, so he took his daughter home.

A few days later the girl developed pleurisy. When he was told of this, Padre Pio exclaimed, "Had she remained at San Giovanni, this would never have happened!"

Her parents called in doctors who were undecided as to what course of action to take. The child was in critical condition, and they feared the worst. At this point a woman, who had been to see Padre Pio, arrived with some articles belonging to the priest. She asked to be allowed to rub the little girl's body with one of them. The parents consented and the little girl fell into a peaceful sleep. When she woke up, her temperature was normal, and Maria felt well. The doctor who attended her checked her temperature again and again, but it remained normal. The astounded doctor had to acknowledge that the fever had gone and his patient was completely cured. "We must also believe in miracles!" he said.

The parents wrote to Padre Pio telling him of the cure and asking if it was time for their daughter to go back to school. "She must wait another twelve days," he told them. This time they obeyed!

In spite of missing fifty-three days of school, due to her illness, Maria finished first in her class. When she and her parents went to thank Padre Pio, he said to the girl, "Thank the Lord who rid you of your cough and cured you again this time. He alone is to be thanked, and no one else."

"Surgical intervention is unnecessary!"

Sometimes, when he knew that God wanted to heal someone, Padre Pio would tell them not to undergo surgery. This was the case for Palma Mannelli.

In June 1940 Palma Mannelli experienced sudden violent pains in her abdomen followed by internal bleeding. She was taken by ambulance to the hospital where the doctors diagnosed her with uterine cancer.

Palma went to Florence for a series of radium treatments. A month later she saw some positive results, but she wondered if they were just temporary. The doctors discharged her and asked her to return a few months later for a checkup.

Palma went back home, but the cancer reappeared. She had two options: She could go back for more treatments or she could have her uterus removed. Her daughter, Liliane, dreamed one night that Padre Pio was repeatedly telling her, "Your mother will get well, and she will get well completely!"

Palma had been advised not to travel, so she asked her husband to go to Padre Pio and plead on her behalf for a cure. He made the trip and spoke twice to Padre Pio about his wife's illness. Padre Pio reassured him, telling him she must take the necessary treatment but on no account should she undergo an operation. "Above all," he said, "no surgeon's knife!"

At this precise moment the woman detected the mysterious perfume, characteristic of Padre Pio. That night Liliane had another dream in which she saw Padre Pio praying before an altar and holding a gold key to his heart. He said to her, "You are not sleeping well are you?" Then after giving her Holy Communion, he led her to a table in the church where there were several pictures of the statue of Our Lady of Grace in the monastery at San Giovanni Rotondo.

Palma returned to Florence for her checkup and underwent extensive examinations. There was no trace of the cancer! She had been completely and definitively cured.

"Come! Come! There's nothing wrong with you!"

In July 1933 Alessandro Galeoti was seized with excruciating stomach pains that affected his breathing and made it impossible to eat. He could only take a few sips of syrup and soft drinks. The family doctor and some excellent specialists could not find the cause of the illness, although they ruled out an ulcer or tumor. The sick man was also unable to sleep.

Alessandro had heard of Padre Pio and he wanted to go to him and ask his intercession with the Lord for a cure. His mother went with him, and they were greeted warmly by Padre Pio, who told them to come back to see him in the afternoon. They went back to the hotel, but the young man's condition worsened. With great effort he went back to the monastery to keep his afternoon appointment.

When Padre Pio saw Alessandro, he went to him, took his hand, and pressed it between his own two wounded hands asking, "Where does it hurt?"

"Father, the pain is here," said the young man, pointing to the spot. "I'm afraid I might have a malignant tumor."

"Come! Come! There's nothing wrong with you!" At that moment, Alessandro sensed a kind of rupture in his body, and he felt much better. His condition improved until, in time, he returned to full health and no longer experienced any pain.

"When the bells ring, you will be healed!"

The following incident took place in 1925 at San Giovanni Rotondo. At the beginning of Holy Week, Mrs. Paolina Preziosi came down with severe bronchitis that developed into pneumonia. The local doctor was called immediately. When he arrived, he quickly saw that nothing could be done for her. This situation was particularly sad because she would leave behind her five children. Her friends and acquaintances, who loved her very much and admired her for the Christian example she gave everyone, went to the monastery and told Padre Pio about Paolina's situation. They begged him to pray to the Lord for her cure.

He listened to them attentively and said, "Tell her not to be afraid because she will rise with the Lord." This meant she would be cured on Holy Saturday when the bells would ring again after the silence of Holy Week.

During the night of Good Friday, when she was praying to God to cure her for the sake of her children, Padre Pio appeared to her and said, "Don't be afraid, creature of God. Hold onto faith and hope, for tomorrow, when the bells ring, you will be cured."

Contrary to these assurances, Mrs. Preziosi went into a coma. Those around her thought the end was near and began making funeral arrangements. Those who had told Padre Pio about her, however, had confidence that things would work out. They went back to the monastery to tell him what was happening and to ask again for his prayers. Padre Pio listened to them, prayed, and then went to the confessional.

A little later he was told that the pastor had given the sacrament of the Sick to the dying woman. Padre Pio went to the altar to begin his Mass. When the bells rang out to announce the Lord's Resurrection, Paolina suddenly shuddered a little and felt her strength return. She got out of bed, where she had been in a coma, and seemed driven by a mysterious force. To the utter astonishment of those around her, of her neighbors, and the whole of San Giovanni Rotondo, she was completely cured! The grace of the Resurrection had come to her house and to her five children.

Someone went to bring the good news to Padre Pio and added, "Perhaps God wanted this woman to be with him, but now she has come back to earth!" The priest replied, "It is also beautiful to be exiled from paradise because of love."

An atheist doctor is cured

At one time, in San Giovanni Rotondo, everyone knew Dr. Francesco Ricciardi. He had been a doctor for some thirty years and devoted himself completely and generously to the care of the sick.

Ricciardi was a frank and honest man, but completely closed to things supernatural. He had never crossed the threshold of a church. He relied completely on science and considered the spiritual and its manifestations as products of the imagination or fanaticism. He had a strong dislike of Padre Pio, whom he considered a dangerous obstacle to the spread of modern knowledge. The people, however, loved their doctor, because he was dedicated to the sick and full of compassion.

He grew old, as we all do, and he began to feel the weight of his years. He also had a serious illness that concerned him greatly and caused him severe stomach pains.

In February 1931 he began to suspect he was gravely ill and sought the opinion of his colleagues. They diagnosed stomach cancer. The doctor had no illusions about the deadly nature of his illness. He knew he was inexorably condemned to death, but he did not know when this would happen. Because he did not have the gift of faith, his sufferings were all the harder to bear.

It was winter, and an icy wind mixed with sleet blew on Mount Gargano. In spite of this, people came to see how Ricciardi was and to bring him the support of their affection and gratitude. One visitor had the idea of bringing the pastor along in case the doctor would be more open to the spiritual. When he saw the priest, Ricciardi ordered him to be thrown out, and the priest had to leave. It was then that the people thought that perhaps Padre Pio might succeed, even if the doctor had been hostile to him in the past. Padre Pio was asked to come to Ricciardi's bedside. It had been ten years since Padre Pio had left the monastery, but on this occasion he went out. As Padre Pio entered the room, his mysterious perfume filled the air, overtaking the bad odor caused by the dying man's disease. The doctor accepted Padre Pio and the notion of the supernatural!

Padre Pio heard Ricciardi's confession and gave him absolution. The doctor's spirit was renewed. To the astonishment of the sick man and those around him, his cancer disappeared, and he was restored to full health and filled with a joy he had never known before.

When the people heard about these wonders, they were overjoyed because their beloved doctor been cured and he had also received the gift of faith.

It happened in a flash!

To save their little girl, who was so gravely ill that the doctors had given up hope, a mother and father went to see Padre Pio to ask his prayers for a cure. They arrived on a Friday. Padre Pio could not receive them because on that day he suffered more than usual from the stigmata and had to stay in bed. The poor parents, anguished by the state of their child's health, did everything possible to see the priest, but in vain.

In great distress they went home without fulfilling the purpose of their visit, *or so they thought!* Someone, however, had told Padre Pio of their plight, and, by using his power of bilocation, he went to the little girl immediately and cured her.

The distraught parents, knowing nothing about this, thought they would find their daughter dying. They were completely surprised when they reached home to see their child running out to greet them, happy and in perfect health! "What did you do to get Padre Pio to visit me so quickly?" the little girl asked. "You had hardly been at San Giovanni Rotondo when he came to cure me!"

It was God's will that this child be cured, so Padre Pio, through his gift of bilocation, arrived where he was needed, like a flash of lightning.

Padre Pio's perfume cures a cancer patient

In October 1949 Maria Rosaria Galiano, who lived in Naples, felt a disturbing pain in her abdomen. After a complete examination, Dr. Battiloro advised her to have her womb tissues tested. Unfortunately this revealed the presence of an adenocarcinoma. This was terrible news for Rosaria and her family because they knew that this was an incurable cancer and would, sooner or later, lead to her death. What were they to do? Attempt an operation perhaps? This might at least put off the fatal hour. Rosaria decided to have the operation with the expected result. She felt some relief initially, but then the cancer reappeared with all its consequences: her pains came back, and her condition worsened.

Her daughter, Rita, had heard about all the good that Padre Pio was able to do for the sick, so she contacted him, first by telephone and then by two letters explaining her mother's condition in detail. The sick woman was in the final stages of her illness, and there was little hope of saving her life. In spite of this and the skepticism of the doctors and those around her, Rita went on believing in Padre Pio.

On the evening of April 29, 1950, Rosaria told Rita that she smelled a strong perfume in her room. Thinking that Rita had sprinkled some eau de cologne, she scolded her. Rita thought her mother was delirious and assured her she had done nothing of the sort. Her mother insisted there was a perfume in her room. The aroma lasted for two days. Rita began to think that this might be the mysterious perfume of Padre Pio, and her hope of a cure grew stronger. On the third day Rosaria felt better and began to sleep, then she started to eat and digest normally and her suffering ended.

She was examined by two doctors. They had to admit, to their surprise, that the cancer had disappeared. After having gone to thank Padre Pio, Rosaria took up her normal life again. Padre Pio's perfume had gone to the very roots of the disease.

Cured in her sleep

Mother Teresa Salvadores, the superior of L'Escuela Taller Medalla Milagrosa, in Montevideo, Uruguay, was dying of stomach cancer and complications associated with it. She was bedridden and could do nothing for herself. Her Sisters had to attend to her every need.

They had heard of Padre Pio and sent him a touching letter begging him to intercede with God for their Superior's cure because they loved her very much and did not want to lose her. Mother Teresa was being kept comfortable with morphine. On the day her letter probably arrived at San Giovanni Rotondo, her condition became so bad that even the morphine had no effect, and death was imminent.

That same day, a relative of Msgr. Damiani, Vicar General of the Diocese of Salto (Uruguay), to whom Padre Pio had given one of his mittens, arrived at the convent. She suggested that it be applied to the ailing parts of Mother Teresa's body. They placed the mitten first on Mother Teresa's side, where there was a swelling the size of a closed fist, and then on her throat, which was tightening up, causing suffocation. She went to sleep after these applications, and she dreamed that Padre Pio came to her, touched her side, and breathed on her mouth.

Three hours later Mother Teresa woke up and, to everyone's amazement, asked for her clothes. She got out of bed, dressed herself, and went to the chapel to pray. At midday she went to the refectory with her community and ate a hearty meal! Her afflictions had gone, and she felt perfectly healthy.

Six months after this sudden and inexplicable cure, she was examined by three doctors, among them a professor from the University of Montevideo. They had to admit that all the stenocardiac symptoms had gone and that Mother Teresa was in excellent health, even if the aortic lesion had not changed. Padre Pio had cured the Superior but had left this mysterious sign for the doctors to discuss among themselves!

He ran away from the hospital

Savinio Greco, an ardent militant communist, lived in the town of Cerignola. It was discovered that he had a brain tumor. He fell into a state of great dejection. He was first hospitalized in Bari and then moved to Milan, where doctors wanted to attempt difficult surgery. During the night the sick man dreamed that Padre Pio came to him, touched his head, and said, "In time you will be cured."

When Greco woke up, he felt cured and wanted to leave the hospital, but the doctors did not believe his story and insisted on going through with the operation. The only option left to Greco was to run away from the hospital. He was caught in Bari and, after some analysis, was put back in the hospital there, where he had first been examined. Before taking him to the operating room, however, the doctors wanted to be sure that there was a tumor, so they examined him again. They had to concede that there was no trace of it! Savinio Greco was able to leave the hospital. Being an honest man, he wanted to pay his bill, but the doctors would not take his money, saying that they had not done anything.

Greco went to San Giovanni Rotondo to thank Padre Pio and to tell him that he would be giving up his communist activities. In the church he was overwhelmed again by an excruciating headache, and he fainted with the pain. He was picked up and revived and taken to Padre Pio. The poor man beseeched the priest, "Father, I have five children and I am seriously ill! Save me! Save my family!"

Padre Pio replied, "I am not God. I am a priest like other priests, no more, no less. I cannot perform miracles."

Then deeply moved with pity for the situation of this unfortunate man, Padre Pio began to pray. As he did so the strong perfume of violets came from him. He said to the man, "Go home and pray. I will also pray and wherever you go my prayers will be with you." At these words Savanio felt his pain leave him, and he was cured again, this time for good!

"Go! Ride your bicycle!"

On getting out of bed on the morning of February 7, 1947, Nicolas De Vincentiis, stationmaster at San Severo, had a bad fall that left him paralyzed.

His family ran to help him and put him onto a chair, then called the doctor. The doctor could not diagnose the cause of the paralysis, and advised that the stationmaster be taken to the neurological clinic in Rome. Here he underwent thorough examinations, but nothing could be done to give him back the use of his legs. He could move a little by using crutches, but he was no longer in control of his body.

The unfortunate De Vincentiis went home very demoralized and began a painful existence, pulling himself around on crutches. He often fell, which aggravated his condition.

After a year of this he decided to go to San Giovanni Rotondo to see Padre Pio. The priest received him with kindness, comforted him, and on taking his leave, said, "Today is Friday. On Monday, take a ride on your bicycle and then make an appointment to be examined again in Rome." De Vincentiis did not understand. Who could ride a bicycle with legs that did not move? "Padre Pio is really odd!" he thought. "Does he realize what a bad state I am in? He seems to. Oh, well, I'll do as he says. Who knows what might happen?"

On Monday De Vincentiis took out his bicycle and tried to get on—and it worked! "Is it possible I am cured?" he asked himself. Then, a few meters further on, he fell. Oh! What is happening? Someone put him back on the bike and yet no one was around! He put his feet on the pedals, and this time everything went well. He wondered what had happened.

We read in the Gospel that St. Peter one day asked Jesus to help him walk on the water of the Lake of Genesareth during a storm. Jesus said to him, "Come!" Peter started out, took fright, and then began to sink. He cried out, "Lord, save me!" The Lord took him by the hand and led him back into the boat, saying, "Man of little faith! Why did you doubt?"

Had something like this happened to De Vincentiis? Probably! The fact is, on that memorable Monday, he recovered the use of his limbs. He returned to Rome for further examinations, and doctors confirmed he was completely cured.

Padre Pio confirms a cure in Switzerland

An engineer named Ferrazzini lived in the canton of Tessin, in Switzerland, with his twenty-one-year-old daughter who had been ill for a long time. Her name was Caterina Maria. One day she asked her father to take her to Padre Pio.

Ferrazzini granted her desire and set out with his daughter for San Giovanni Rotondo. It was a long journey, and when they finally arrived they took rooms in a hotel. At this point something very unusual happened. As soon as she arrived in San Giovanni, Caterina's suffering ceased!

The next day she went to see Padre Pio who heard her confession and gave her his blessing. A few days later Caterina and her father decided to go back to Switzerland. The young girl continued to be in good health. On their return the doctor who had been treating her advised a checkup, and Caterina went to the hospital for further examinations, while her father went back to work.

One morning, when taking out his car to go to his office, he saw Padre Pio near the garage. He took him to be his pastor but then quickly realized he was a Capuchin. Astonished he asked Padre Pio, "Father, what are you doing here?"

"I have come to see how you are," Padre Pio replied.

"Very well, Father," said Ferrazzini, "although, we are still a little concerned about Caterina. The results of her tests at the hospital have still to come through."

"Don't worry," Padre Pio said, "everything will be all right." He gave his blessing and disappeared.

Ferrazzini was astounded but also encouraged by the priest's words. The results of Caterina's tests were, in fact, positive. Padre Pio, through his mysterious gift of bilocation, had come to confirm the cure that had taken place earlier in San Giovanni Rotondo and to bring Ferrazzini the comfort of his presence.

"Is Padre Pio mistaken?"

Giuseppina Marchetti was living with her father in Bologna in July 1930. She was twenty-four and some years earlier had been in an accident that resulted in a badly broken right arm. She had undergone an operation. Three years later, another operation proved unsuccessful. Because of this she had to undergo a series of very painful treatments. After another examination the surgeon told her she would never recover the use of her arm because a bone graft had not taken. Father and daughter were quite desolate.

What should they do? An idea came to mind.

They knew Padre Pio and had confidence in him. Since modern science could do nothing, why not ask Padre Pio to intercede with God for a cure?

At San Giovanni Rotondo, Padre Pio greeted them with affection and encouraged them to trust in God and not to give up. Giuseppina would definitely be cured! He blessed them and took his leave.

The days went by and nothing happened. What was going on? Was Padre Pio mistaken? No, not at all. He had foreseen a long delay in the young girl's cure. Of course, the father and daughter knew nothing of this and went back to Bologna rather puzzled.

On September 17, 1930, feast of the Stigmata of St. Francis, the Marchetti house was pervaded by the scents of jonquils and roses, and this lasted about fifteen minutes. It was the mysterious mark of Padre Pio, who kept his promise.

Giuseppina's arm was healed. She realized very quickly that her arm was normal again, and this was confirmed later by the x-rays.

A cure during confession

One day, the playwright Luigi Antonelli told a journalist of his extraordinary cure through the intervention of Padre Pio. His doctors had found a cancer covering the area between his ear and his shoulder. They had spoken to him about having an operation. He went to a surgeon and asked him, "How much time have I got left?"

The surgeon replied, "With the operation six months, and without it, three months."

"All right," said Antonelli, "I'll have the operation. I can't turn down an extra three months of life!"

And he would have undergone the operation had not one of his friends advised him to go to San Giovanni Rotondo and see Padre Pio. Perhaps the priest would ask the Lord to cure him without the operation. Antonelli reflected on this, then said, "Why not?" He set out for San Giovanni, and when he arrived went immediately to the little church and attended Padre Pio's Mass. Afterward, he went to confession.

What happened during this confession? Antonelli found it difficult to describe even though he was a man who had a way with words. During confession he had a long conversation with Padre Pio, and the longer it went on, the more his soul was transported into a celestial state. At the same time he felt a kind of current circulating in his body, eradicating all traces of the cancer.

When he got off his knees, Antonelli felt in good health. His soul as well as his body had been cured. He took up all his activities again without ever experiencing again the slightest symptoms of cancer.

"He is the one I saw!"

Concetta Bellarmini was a pharmacist. In 1926 she contracted a blood infection and then bronchial pneumonia. She was reduced to a wretched state. Her skin was yellow. The doctors were unable to do anything for her, so one of her relatives suggested that the sick woman should have recourse to Padre Pio, whom she had never met. Her children were against this because they did not believe in anything done by this friar from Gargano. But Concetta did not agree with them, and with great fervor invoked Padre Pio.

One day, when she was in bed, a Capuchin appeared in her room. Without touching her, he smiled and blessed her. She was not afraid of this apparition but felt serene and peaceful afterward. She asked him if his coming meant the grace of conversion for her children or her cure. The friar answered, "On Sunday morning you will return to good health." He then disappeared leaving behind an intense perfume that her servant also noticed.

When Sunday came, Concetta realized she had been cured, and her skin had regained its normal coloring. She then wanted to go to San Giovanni Rotondo to meet Padre Pio and thank him. Her brother went with her on this journey. When they arrived at the monastery, they asked which friar was Padre Pio. Someone pointed him out when he came through the crowd. Concetta Bellarmini recognized in him the Capuchin who had appeared to her in her room at Lanciano, and she cried out, "That's him! He is the one I saw!"

A new lease on life

Maria-Silvia, the three-year-old daughter of Dr. Gaetano Benini, who practiced medicine in Fontignano, was taken to a hospital in Perugia on October 15, 1952. A final attempt was to be made to remove a cancer of the intestines. The operation, undertaken by distinguished surgeons, colleagues of Dr. Benini, was unsuccessful. He was resigned to taking his daughter home to die with her family. Five days later, however, she had a dream in which she saw the child Jesus accompanied by Padre Pio.

The child Jesus came to her and told her to let her parents know that they need not worry because Padre Pio had asked for and obtained her cure. The little girl told all this to her mother and father when she awoke. She then got up and said she wanted to go play with her friends. The parents were beside themselves with joy and could hardly believe what had happened, but the facts were there! Her father went off to San Giovanni Rotondo to thank Padre Pio. The priest welcomed him warmly and assured him that his little daughter was indeed cured. He also encouraged the doctor to be more attentive to his Christian duties.

Padre Pio and Giovannino

Gino was a dock worker in the port of Naples. He was active in the Communist Party and had great dreams for the future of the Marxist revolution. But as we say, "Don't count your chickens before they're hatched!"

One day he fell in love with a young girl named Francesca, and he wanted to marry her. But she did not share his Marxist opinions. He was determined to marry her all the same and would try to find a way.

Alas! Francesca had an accident that affected her ability to have children. Still, Gino was determined to marry her because he loved her very much. A short time later they were married. Soon Gino and Francesca were expecting a baby. Then the trouble began! Because of the consequences of her accident, the doctors feared she would not be able to give birth without endangering her own life. A choice had to be made between saving the baby or the mother. Francesca fell into a deep despondency. What should she do? Have an abortion? While she was thinking about this dilemma, a Capuchin appeared unexpectedly in her room. He stood at the foot of her bed and said, "You must not do any such thing! You will have this child, and it will be a boy, and you will call him Giovanni."

Francesca had never seen Padre Pio, but when she saw a photograph of him later, she recognized the Capuchin who had come to her room. Assured by his visit, she was no longer in doubt. She would have the baby! Her parents were very much against her decision and could not believe it. She remained adamant and brought the baby into the world without any complications. Those who had warned her had to accept the evidence. The baby was baptized Giovanni. Gino, his father, confused by all this, had to face reality.

Padre Pio had opened a road to him somewhat different from that of the Marxist revolution. When Gino went with his wife to thank Padre Pio, he promised that they would walk, with Giovanni, on the road of a fervent Christian life.

"She is better off in heaven!"

Father Alberto D'Apolito recounts that, one day, he received a telegram from a rich industrialist living in Piedmont. This man was a spiritual son of Padre Pio. He was asking Father D'Apolito to solicit Padre Pio's prayer for his wife, who was dying from an internal hemorrhage. He added that if his wife was cured he would give a large donation to the Casa Sollievo della Sofferenza.

Father D'Apolito passed on his friend's request to Padre Pio. Obviously moved, the priest assured him he would pray for the sick woman.

When, however, he heard there was a question of money being given if the cure happened, he changed his mind and said to Father D'Apolito, "We don't make deals with the Lord!" He added, "But, I will pray for the salvation of her soul." When he said this, there were signs of great suffering on his face. At that very moment the industrialist's wife died, assisted by a priest.

A few days later, when Father D'Apolito told Padre Pio about her death, he cried out, "She is better off in heaven!"

"Woman! Why do you besiege me?"

A woman from San Giovanni watched her sick husband go from bad to worse and sink rapidly toward death. In great distress, she ran to the monastery to get Padre Pio to pray for his recovery. There was such a large crowd around the priest that she could not get near him.

What should she do? Speak to him in confession?

A long line of people were waiting for confession, so she would be the last in line. In deep thought she prayed interiorly that Padre Pio would help her husband who, at any moment, might die and leave her alone to bring up their children.

When she saw Padre Pio go the altar to celebrate Mass, she dashed over there, but the crowd was just as large, and she could not even see the priest! She tried going to the right, then the left, but it was no use. She could only go on praying, interiorly, filled with an anguish that wrenched her heart, because the inevitable could happen to her husband at any moment.

When Padre Pio finished Mass, the poor woman managed to squeeze into the corridor he used to go to the monastery. There she went on praying in her heart. Padre Pio came along and stopped by her, saying, "Woman of little faith! Why do you besiege and bombard me with your prayer? Do you think I'm deaf? You have already told me what you want, five times, from the right and left, from in front and behind! I have understood! I get the message! Go home! Everything is all right!"

Full of joy, the woman thanked him and ran home as if she had wings on her feet. She arrived at her house, breathless, to find her husband in perfect health.

Padre Pio's healing scarf

Guiseppe Canaponi tells how, in the winter of 1954, he arrived at San Giovanni Rotondo during a storm. He had to walk a good part of the road to the monastery in the pouring rain and arrived cold and soaked to the skin. He had also lost his voice! Because he was a close friend of Padre Pio's, he went straight up to the friar's cell and found the priest in conversation with the Superior.

Canaponi greeted them both with his barely audible voice. Seeing him in such a sorry state, Padre Pio asked what had happened. He then touched Canaponi and said, "My poor friend, you are soaked through!" He turned to the Superior and asked, "Is there anything we can put around his shoulders to warm him?" The Superior did not have anything at hand. Then Padre Pio searched around his cell and finally found a large brown scarf hanging behind the door. "Lucky for you!" he said to Canaponi. "It is almost new. I have hardly worn it!" He then tied it around the man's neck. Canaponi felt a great warmth surge through his body and exclaimed, "I feel better already!"

And in saying this he realized his voice had come back to normal. "You see," said Padre Pio simply, "the warmth has done you good!"

"Do not move before Sunday!"

There was a young woman in San Giovanni Rotondo who often went to the monastery and to Padre Pio's Mass. She contracted a leg infection that kept her in bed for a long time. This meant she could not go to the monastery. She did everything she could to get well and to shorten her stay in bed, but the leg was healing very slowly. She grew impatient and one day got out of bed. She had a bad fall, and her leg swelled up.

She had someone ask Padre Pio to pray for her because she was tired of waiting and wanted to go to Mass the following Sunday. Padre Pio replied, "It will be all right for Sunday. She will go to Mass, but she must not move before then!" To the astonishment of her doctor, the young woman was completely healed and went to Mass the following Sunday.

"I will come with you."

An engineer from Rome named Todini, who had come to visit Padre Pio, stayed with him long into the evening. Because it was late, Todini wanted to get back to his hotel. When he opened the monastery door, he saw it was raining very heavily, and he had not brought an umbrella. What was to be done? It was a two-kilometer walk between the monastery and his hotel, and in such heavy rain he would be soaked through and risk catching cold. He asked Padre Pio if there was any chance he could spend the night at the monastery. Padre Pio said it was impossible. He told him to go back to his hotel without worrying about the rain as he would accompany him. Todini was not quite sure what this meant, but set out all the same.

A wonderful thing happened! The rain stopped suddenly and not one drop fell on Todini all the way from the monastery to the hotel. When he got there, the receptionist was very surprised he had walked back in such a downpour, assuming that he must be soaked through. Todini assured her that he was not wet and that, in fact, he was quite dry, and invited her to touch him to make sure! She did so and saw that he was indeed dry. She looked outside. The rain was still pouring down as it had been for over an hour. She could not understand. "What did you do to stay so dry?" she asked.

The engineer replied, "Padre Pio said he would come with me, and, as you can see, he kept the rain off me!"

The woman exclaimed, "Padre Pio's company is certainly more effective than all the umbrellas in the world!"

"It is not yet time to go."

At the monastery in San Giovanni Rotondo lived a friar named Brother Léon de Tora. He had been sick for a long time with a painful illness that caused him great suffering. Whenever Padre Pio returned to his cell after confessions, he never forgot to visit Brother Léon, inquire about his health, and comfort him in his sufferings.

One day, as usual, Padre Pio went to see the sick Brother with some of his confreres, among them Brother Daniel, whom he had saved from certain death after much prayer and a great deal of suffering offered on his behalf. Padre Pio went over to the bed and asked Brother Léon how he was feeling. At the same time, Padre Pio unbuttoned the Brother's shirt and placed on the sick man's neck one of the mittens he wore to cover the stigmata.

Brother Léon felt he could not endure any more suffering and said to Padre Pio, "I want to die!"

"Brother," said Padre Pio, "your train ticket is not yet ready!" And he left the room.

As Brother Daniel followed Padre Pio to his cell, he asked, "What about me, Father, wasn't my ticket ready?"

"Yes!" he replied. "Not only was your ticket ready, but the train as well! You will never know how much you cost me!"

"Don't say anything to anyone!"

Father Placido of San Marco in Lamis was a confrère of Padre Pio's. They had been through the novitiate and studies together. In July 1957 Father Placido fell seriously ill with cirrhosis of the liver and was taken to a hospital in San Severo.

One night, he saw Padre Pio standing near him, encouraging him and assuring him that he would recover. Padre Pio then went over to the window, put his hand on the glass, and disappeared.

The next morning Father Placido experienced a great feeling of well-being throughout his body and got out of bed. He went to the window and saw the imprint of Padre Pio's hand on the glass. The news of this traveled fast around the hospital, and people flocked to his room to see the imprint for themselves. Of course, the news spread outside the hospital too, and people came in off the streets, so there was a lot of coming and going; this upset the hospital's routine. The hospital authorities had to intervene. Other people just laughed at such a ridiculous happening, but Father Placido kept on insisting that Padre Pio had come and had left the imprint of his hand on the window. They tried to clean off the imprint, but it would not wash away and remained there for some time.

Father Alberto D'Apolito, who was in San Severo at the time, visited the hospital and saw this phenomenon for himself. He wanted to be sure that Padre Pio had, in fact, come to the hospital. So, on his next visit to San Giovanni, he asked him. Padre Pio replied, "Yes, I went to the hospital, but don't say anything to anyone!"

CHAPTER 7

Appeals from Beyond the Grave

The aim of Christian life is to be with God forever. To reach this goal, Christians must prepare themselves in this world, so that they may be worthy to be with God.

Many do not think of this preparation, and others do not get the time; their lives are cut off when they least expect it. This means that, after death, some have more preparation to do before reaching the vision of God.

It would seem that God sometimes allows certain souls to ask for help from those still on earth. Padre Pio received many such requests from these "beggars" beyond the grave, although he did not often speak about this. He has, however, left an impressive account, including the following occurrences.

Four deceased friars visit the monastery

Padre Pio told this story one evening in February 1922 to the *fratini*, young boys educated by the Capuchins:

"Listen and I will tell you what happened to me a few days ago. I came down one night to warm myself at the fireplace in the community room and was surprised to find four friars sitting beside the fire in silence and with their cowls pulled down. I greeted them, as we usually do, with 'Praised be Jesus Christ!' but no one responded. Astonished, I looked at them closely to find out who they were, but I did not recognize any of them. I stood there for several minutes watching them, and it seemed to me they were in some kind of pain. I greeted them again, but there was no response.

"I then went off to find out if we had some visiting friars staying with us. Father Superior said to me, 'Padre Pio, who would venture up here in such terrible weather?' I said to him, 'But Father Guardian, downstairs around our fire there are four Capuchins sitting on the benches, with their cowls pulled down, warming themselves. I greeted them, but they did not answer, and I did not recognize them when I looked closely. I don't know who they are!'

"Father Guardian exclaimed, 'Is it possible that some visiting Brothers have arrived without anyone letting me know? Let's go and see!'

"When we got there we did not find anyone by the fire! I understood then, that they must have been dead religious who were undergoing their purgatory here, where they had offended God. I spent the whole night before the Blessed Sacrament, praying for their deliverance."

The old man who was burned alive

Padre Pio told the following story one afternoon in May 1922 to Bishop Alberto Costa of Melfi:

"We were in the middle of World War II, and the monastery at San Giovanni Rotondo, like all other monasteries at the time, was rather empty. The friars had been called up to serve in the army. The Seraphic College was moved to the monastery, and Father Paolino da Casacalenda and I were in charge. One winter afternoon, Assunta Di Tommaso, Father Paolino's sister, arrived at the monastery. She had come to visit her brother for a few days. There was thick snow everywhere. Father Paolina advised his sister to make her way to the village before nightfall and to stay with Rachelina Russo, a benefactor of the monastery.

"Assunta refused to go out alone in such deep snow, afraid she might meet with a stray and hungry wolf or be attacked by some marauder. Father Paolino reminded her that the rules of enclosure did not allow women to enter the cloister. What was to be done? 'Make up a bed here in this room just for tonight,' Assunta said, 'and I will go to Rachelina tomorrow.' 'Good!' said Father Paolino. 'If you are happy to spend the night here, I will have a bed made up for you and you can sleep here in peace.'

"He called some of the boys to make up a camp bed and light a fire in the room. After supper, when the boys were in bed, Father Paolino and I went down to see Assunta. Some time later, Father Paolina said to his sister, 'I am going to say a Rosary in the church. You can stay and chat with Padre Pio.'

"She said she would rather go with him, so they went off together.

"On leaving, they closed the door and I sat alone by the fire. I was praying, with my eyes half-closed, when the door opened and an old man came in dressed in the kind of cloak worn by the peasants of San Giovanni Rotondo. He sat down beside me. I looked at him and wondered how he had got into the monastery at this hour. 'Who are you and what do you want?' I asked him. 'Padre Pio,' he replied. 'I am Pietro Di Mauro, son of the late Nicolas, nicknamed, Precoco. I died in this monastery on September 18, 1908, in cell number 4, when there used to be a shelter for beggars here. One night I fell asleep in bed smoking a cigarette. I set fire to the mattress, and I was suffocated and burned to death. I am still in purgatory, and I need one Mass for my deliverance. The Lord has allowed me to ask your help.' I told him to be at peace and that I would say a Mass the next day, for his deliverance.

"I got up and walked him to the monastery door to let him out. I saw that the door was locked and barred. I opened it, and the old man left. The moon was shining brightly on the snow-covered square. It was almost as clear as day. When I could not see the old man anymore, I felt a kind of fear, closed the door, and went back to the room, trembling.

"Father Paolino and his sister returned after reciting the Rosary. When they saw how pale and ashen I looked, they thought I was sick. Having said good night to his sister, Father Paolino walked me to my cell. I did not say a word about the dead man.

"A few days after Assunta left, Father Paolino wanted to know what had happened the night I did not feel well. I told him in great detail of my encounter with this apparition from beyond the grave, and added, 'I couldn't say in front of your sister that the dead had visited me, because she would not have slept in that room!'"

Father Paolino wanted to check out what the beggar had told Padre Pio. He went to the City Hall, where the registers confirmed everything the beggar had told Padre Pio.

The novice in the unlit church

Another incident concerned the apparition of a novice. Padre Pio was praying one night in the sanctuary when he heard a noise near the altar. Thinking that someone had come into the church with evil intent, he called out, "Who's there?" There was no response.

He went back to his prayer, thinking that it had been the wind, but he heard the noise again. Padre Pio went over to the choir grill and looked toward the high altar. There he saw a young novice cleaning.

"What are you doing over there?" Padre Pio asked.

"I'm cleaning," replied the novice.

"But," asked Padre Pio, "how can you do that in the dark?"

The young man replied, "I am a Capuchin novice doing my purgatory here, and I need help." Then, he disappeared!

Next day, Padre Pio came to his aid by celebrating Mass for him.

All his illnesses were over!

Padre Pio related the following incident to Father Bernardo d'Apicella. On December 29, 1936, Father Giacinto of Sant'Elia in Pianisi came from Foggia to San Giovanni Rotondo to ask prayers for the dying Father Giuseppantonio of San Marco in Lamis.

Padre Pio assured Father Giacinto that he would pray for the dying man. He spent that day and the next going about his priestly duties. That night Padre Pio went to his cell and was preparing for bed when he saw Father Giuseppantonio standing in front of him. Surprised, Padre Pio asked him, "How did you get here? I was told you are very seriously ill, and yet, here you are!" Father Giuseppantonio made a sign indicating that he was dead and also to let him know that all his illnesses were over!

A friend visits from beyond the grave

On March 7, 1988, I was passing by Trevi, the home of the Marchioness Giovanna Boschi of whom I wrote earlier. I stopped by to find out about an apparition the Marchioness had had of her friend, Marguerite Hamilton, three days after the friend's death. She gave me the following details.

Marguerite had confided to her friend that, during her last confession with Padre Pio, he had assured her he would be with her at the moment of her death and bless her three times.

One day in 1974, Marguerite said to the Marchioness, "Padre Pio often appears in dreams to other people, but not to me!" On April 29, 1974, however, she told her friend, Giovanna, "Tonight, Padre Pio appeared to me in a dream, and blessed me three times. The hour of my death is at hand."

The Marchioness told her it was only a dream and that she should not take it so seriously. The two friends made a pact that whoever died first should, God willing, come back and tell the other about her state in the next world. That same afternoon the Marchioness went to see Marguerite, who had calmed down a bit, so that they could talk together again of the dream, and she could give her some comfort. While they were talking, Marguerite went white, collapsed, and died of a stroke. Giovanna was overcome with emotion and grief.

Three days after the funeral, while the Marchioness was resting on her bed saying the Rosary, she saw Marguerite sitting in her husband Fernando's armchair! She thought this must be a hallucination and, rubbing her eyes, looked again and again. Her friend was still there and a light shone from her. Finally, the Marchioness took her courage in both hands and asked if she was her friend Marguerite. "Yes!" replied the woman in the armchair. It was indeed Marguerite who had come back to tell her that Padre Pio had assisted her in her last moments and that she was safe and happy. She then disappeared.

CHAPTER 8

Padre Pio's Familiarity with His Guardian Angel

For most of us, our guardian angels are a great unknown. For Padre Pio, on the contrary, his guardian angel was well-known and worked with the friar on his sanctification and in his priestly ministry. Between them there was a kind of bond. You could almost say they lived together.

The very exceptional, spiritual life of Padre Pio necessitated exceptional assistance on the part of his guardian angel. Again, his priestly ministry, replete with so many charisms, demanded a great deal of this help, in a variety of ways, such as being a messenger to people in touch with Padre Pio, translating foreign languages, and so on. Here are some glimpses of this familiarity between Padre Pio and his guardian angel.

Padre Pio reproaches his guardian angel

Once, Padre Pio was violently attacked by the devil and his cohort, whom he called "cossacks." The struggle was so intense that at one point Padre Pio thought he was lost, so he called out to his guardian angel for help. But the angel did not come, and Padre Pio had to fight alone. As usual, though, Padre Pio threw himself completely into the struggle and prayed with greater intensity than ever. In the end he came out victorious but exhausted.

Then the angel appeared. Padre Pio was really angry with him and reproached him for not coming when he called urgently for his help. Then, as if he wanted to "punish" the angel, Padre Pio turned away without even looking at him. The angel followed him looking dejected and nearly in tears!

Eventually, when they were reconciled the angel explained it was not negligence that had kept him away, but God had wanted Padre Pio to come through this battle unaided.

Padre Pio speaks English

Angelina Sorritelli, daughter of an Italian emigrant to the United States, was born in America and spoke only English. Her father, Tommaso, took her to San Giovanni Rotondo because he wanted Padre Pio to hear her confession and give her First Communion.

At this time, Maria Pyle, an American, was living in a house near the monastery, and she helped in Padre Pio's work. As soon as she heard the girl had arrived, she offered her services as interpreter to Angelina. When she offered Padre Pio her services, he thanked her but said he would deal with Angelina directly. Amazed, Miss Pyle withdrew, and Padre Pio heard the little girl's confession.

When it was over, Miss Pyle asked the child, "Did you understand what Padre Pio said?"

"Yes," the girl said.

"And he understood you?" Miss Pyle asked.

"Yes," the girl answered again.

"And what did he speak, English?" Miss Pyle went on.

"Yes," said the girl, "he spoke in English."

Padre Pio speaks German

Professor Bruno Rabajotti recounts how he was in Padre Pio's cell, reciting the Rosary with him. When they had finished, someone brought in a German visitor, a tall, thin man with short white hair. He began to thank Padre Pio, in German, for the wonderful things that had happened to his daughter.

The conversation continued for a while with questions and answers between the two men. Rabajotti could hardly believe his ears. Padre Pio was speaking German and looked over at him, from time to time, with a twinkle in his eye! Eventually, Padre Pio said to him, "You seem surprised to hear me speak and understand a language I don't know. I am not the only one who can do that. Why don't you try?"

"But I don't know any German, Father!"

"Neither do I," the priest said, "but it is easy. All you have to do is begin speaking. This man, who came here a year ago, will tell you his story. Differences of language and barriers between souls disappear when we speak the only language that really matters, that of the spirit."

Professor Rabajotti did as Padre Pio told him, and to his utter amazement he was able to hold a conversation with the man in German! During this time, Padre Pio stood watching them with his arms crossed, absolutely delighted.

The professor went on to say, "Although we spoke in German, I thought I was speaking Italian. It was so easy and so beautiful. Before leaving we embraced."

An unusual mail carrier

Cleonice Morcaldi, a woman from San Giovanni Rotondo, told us a strange story. During World War II, one of her nephews was taken prisoner. For over a year the family had no news of him. They suspected the worst. One day, Cleonice went to Padre Pio, threw herself at his feet, and begged him to tell her at least whether her nephew was alive or dead!

The priest reassured her and said, "Get up and go in peace." Even if his words gave her hope, she was still full of doubts. The days passed and no news came. Her anxiety increased all the more. Finally, she decided to try something, even if it seemed a bit foolish! Sustained by her great faith, she went back to Padre Pio and said to him, "Let's try this. I will write a letter to my nephew, but I can only put his name on the envelope, because I don't know where he is. It's up to you and your guardian angel to see that he gets it!" Padre Pio said nothing, but Cleonice thought to herself that silence means consent. Her hope was renewed.

That night, she wrote the letter before going to sleep and put it on the bedside table. The next morning, her surprise was mixed with fear when she noticed the letter had disappeared. She ran to Padre Pio who said to her, "Thank the Blessed Virgin!"

Fifteen days later, she received a reply to her letter. In it she read the good news that Giovannino was alive. He enclosed his address, saying he would see her again soon.

A spiritual daughter makes herself heard

When Padre Pio was forbidden to write to his spiritual sons and daughters, some asked him: "Father, what are we going to do since you cannot write to us?" He replied, "Send your guardian angel instead!"

Rachelina, one of Padre Pio's spiritual daughters who actively helped in his work and enterprises, was fully aware that Padre Pio was forbidden to keep in touch with the outside world. In spite of that, she insisted on seeing Padre Pio, because she urgently needed to speak with him for the good of her soul. Padre Pio replied that, because he was anxious to obey the orders he had received, he could not come to the parlor.

This woman, who was more concerned about her personal needs than about Padre Pio's situation, was very annoyed and complained of being treated in this way, especially after all she had done for the priest and the monastery. Back home, she told her guardian angel to let Padre Pio know she would not be at Mass or Communion the next day.

Evidently, the guardian angel had carried out her order because, that very evening, Padre Pio replied, "Tell Rachelina not to go to Communion tomorrow!"

The next day, Rachelina, nevertheless, went to the monastery to work as usual with her colleague, Lucietta Fiorentino. While she was working, Padre Pio appeared and said, "Bravo! Your guardian angel is your messenger. At your imperious command he brought me all your rage!" He then turned to Lucietta and said, "Do you know, Lucietta, what this woman has done? Out of anger, she decided she would not go to Mass or Holy Communion, then she arrogantly commanded her guardian angel to let me know!"

Rachelina was greatly embarrassed and asked, "Father, did my guardian angel really go and tell you everything?"

"Of course, he did," Padre Pio answered. "He is not disobedient like you!"

Padre Pio's considerate guardian angel

At one time, Padre Pio was ill and had to keep to his bed. Father Paolino da Casacalenda, his Superior, often came to see him. One night the Superior said to Padre Pio, "Father, if you need me during the night, send your guardian angel." Padre Pio said he would certainly do so.

Father Paolino went to bed. Around midnight his bed was violently shaken. Half awake, he knew that Padre Pio's guardian angel had come for him, but he was so overcome by fatigue and drowsiness that he fell back into a deep sleep.

The next morning he told Padre Pio what had happened and how mortified he felt about not coming to him. He suggested that, next time, the guardian angel should shake the bed a little harder. That night the guardian angel came and shook the bed very strongly, but again, the priest could not wake up completely and fell back asleep.

Feeling more and more humiliated by all this, the Superior went to Padre Pio and said he should ask his guardian angel to treat him less delicately, otherwise the Superior would never wake up. The angel must really shake the bed in such a way that he would be up and running to Padre Pio.

On the third night, the guardian angel came and shook the bed so violently that the priest leapt out and ran to ask what Padre Pio wanted. The priest said to him, "I am in a sweat! Help me change my clothes, please, as I cannot do it myself."

CHAPTER 9

On First-Name Terms with the Devil, Barbablù!

A priest like Padre Pio, destined by the Lord to do great things for the glory of God and the salvation of souls, could not escape the fierce opposition of the sworn enemy of God and man—the devil. Padre Pio nicknamed him "Barbablù" ("Bluebeard"). Padre Pio had to confront the devil from his very first steps on the road to sanctity and kept up a continual and particularly terrifying battle with him.

This hard-fought battle cost him great sacrifices and had severe physical consequences, but Padre Pio always won! Here are some encounters in this war between Padre Pio and Satan.

A ferocious dog

The following episode was told by Padre Pio himself in a letter written to Father Agostino, his spiritual director.

"It happened when I was studying philosophy at Sant'Elia in Pianisi. I had the second to last cell in the corridor leading to the church, at about the height of the statue of the Immaculate Conception over the high altar.

"One night, after Matins, I had opened the door and the window because the heat was unbearable. Suddenly I heard noises apparently coming from the cell next door and wondered what Brother Atanasio could be doing at that hour. Thinking he was keeping a prayer vigil, I began to recite the Rosary. We had challenged each other to see who could pray the most, and I did not want to be left behind! But the noises continued and grew louder, and I wanted to call my confrere. There was a strong smell of sulfur. I leaned out the window to call him. (Our windows were so close we could easily pass something from one to the other.) 'Brother Atanasio! Brother Atanasio!' I called, without raising my voice too much. As there was no response, I came away from the window, but to my horror, I saw a huge dog, smoke pouring from its jaws, come through the door. I fell back on my bed and heard it say, 'He is the one! He is the one!' Still lying there, I watched this horrible beast leap onto the opposite roof and disappear."

The next day, Padre Pio learned that Brother Atanasio had not been in his cell because he was away from the monastery. Padre Pio then tried to find out from the local people who owned this animal, but no one could tell him. He was then convinced that the devil had come in the guise of this beast and that he would continue to come day and night in one form or another.

During these apparitions, the devil nearly always took forms that were obscene, bestial, or monstrous. At times he would take angelic forms and even appeared in the form of St.

Francis, the Blessed Virgin, and Christ himself! Padre Pio wrote:

"Barbablù does not want to admit defeat! He has taken every imaginable form. For several days he visited me with his helpers, armed with sticks and iron instruments and, what is worse, looking ugly and horrible. The last night was the worst. This 'cossack' kept striking me, from about ten o'clock at night, when I usually go to bed, until five o'clock in the morning. He made diabolical suggestions to me, for example, thoughts of despair and giving up my trust in God. I thought this must be the last night of my life or that I would go off my head. But, praised be to Jesus, nothing like this happened. However, at five o'clock in the morning, when the 'cossack' left, a chill spread all over my body, and I began to shake like a reed in the wind. This lasted two hours and I spat up blood."

A bogus confessor

Padre Pio was ill one day in the monastery at Venafro. Suddenly the door opened and someone came in who looked like Padre Pio's confessor, Father Agostino da San Marco in Lamis. This was the devil. He came over to Padre Pio and said he had come to hear his confession. Padre Pio looked at him closely and saw that he did, indeed, look like Father Agostino, but he was not completely convinced, as he found something strange about his face.

Moreover, he experienced this nausea whenever the devil was present. To make sure it was Father Agostino, he exclaimed, "Say, 'Jesus Christ forever!'" At that moment, the false Father Agostino yelled, "No!" and immediately disappeared.

From disbelief to terror

Padre Pio had to deal with the devil over a long period of time, and he became used to his apparitions, his harassments, and the struggles out of which the priest always emerged victorious, even if physically he was left in bad shape.

After many months in his home village of Pietrelcina, in the Province of Benevento, where he was trying to recover his health, Padre Pio received orders to go to the monastery of Sant'Anna in Foggia.

With his arrival, the monastery lost its customary peace because the devil followed Padre Pio to his new home. Every night, at the same time, strange noises could be heard, culminating in a loud explosion. Padre Pio was tempted in every way, attacked, mistreated, dragged from one place to another in an indescribable uproar. When the devil saw he could not win, he released Padre Pio with an infernal noise.

Padre Pio's confreres were afraid and upset by all this. They hoped it would end soon. On the contrary, to everyone's consternation, it continued.

One day, Andrea D'Agostino, Bishop of Ariano Irpino, arrived at the monastery and asked for hospitality.

In the course of conversation, mention was made of the terrible noises that came from Padre Pio's cell when he was fighting the devil. The bishop listened, but made light of it, saying that, in his opinion, this was utter nonsense and should not be believed. That very night, however, he was forced to change his mind! The bishop was so terrified he wanted to leave the monastery immediately, but it was only two in the morning, and there were no means of transportation. He had to stay, but he insisted that a friar remain in the room with him throughout the rest of the night! The next morning the bishop left very quickly and with very different ideas from those he had had the night before! Seeing, or rather hearing, is believing!

"*Stay awhile!*"

At the monastery of Sant'Anna in Foggia, Padre Pio had a confrère named Brother Francesco de Torremaggiore. He often went to Padre Pio's cell in the evening to keep him company. Padre Pio appreciated this very much because, as long as Brother Francesco was there, the "cossacks" did not come.

One night, as usual, Brother Francesco went up to Padre Pio's cell for a chat. That night, however, Brother Francesco was very tired and kept dropping off to sleep. Eventually he stood up and made as if to leave, but Padre Pio said to him, "Stay a while, because if you don't they—the 'cossacks'—will come." So Brother Francesco stayed a bit longer, although he was very drowsy. Finally, he said he really had to go, because he could not stay awake any longer. "Go, Brother, go!" said Padre Pio.

Brother Francesco had hardly taken ten steps when he heard the most terrible noise coming from Padre Pio's cell. He went straight back and found Padre Pio completely exhausted and soaked in sweat from the struggle he had with the demons. They had come as usual to attack Padre Pio, taking advantage of Brother Francesco's departure.

"*You will not hear it again.*"

All this noise, night after night, eventually tried the patience of the friars beyond endurance, especially one of them, who was kind and understanding, but always on edge and on the verge of a nervous breakdown. One evening, when he was in the refectory with the others, the terrible noises started again, above his head, where Padre Pio's room was located. In a fit of anger, the nervous friar yelled, "Is this never going to end?"

This was reported to Padre Pio who said in a resigned way, "They must not hear this again." He prayed to the Lord for this intention and, from that time on, the friars heard no further noise.

This did not mean, however, that the devil ceased to torment Padre Pio. On the contrary, the priest had to carry this terrible cross alone.

Interference with the mail

When Padre Pio was living in Pietrelcina for the good of his health, he kept up a correspondence with his spiritual director, Father Agostino. But he was, at the same time, under the immediate direction of the archpriest, Father Salvatore Pannullo, who was quick to realize that he was dealing with a special penitent. He took every precaution to make sure his people would not be misled by this extraordinary man.

As one of these precautions, he had agreed with Padre Pio that each letter sent by Father Agostino should be shown to him first. One day, Padre Pio received a letter and brought it to Father Salvatore. When he opened it, he found a blank sheet of paper inside.

He said to Padre Pio, "Father Agostino must have made a mistake and put this blank paper in the envelope instead of a letter."

"Father Agostino did not make a mistake," Padre Pio said. "There is writing on it, but Barbablù has made it illegible."

Father Salvatore exclaimed, "So *you* know what is written there?"

"Yes, I know," said Padre Pio, and repeated all that Father Agostino had written.

Father Salvatore was taken aback by this. To check the truth of the matter, he wrote, with haste, to Father Agostino to see if he had really written what Padre Pio had said. Father Agostino confirmed this, word for word!

Another time, a letter arrived, but, in the middle of the paper was a large stain, shaped like a funnel, making it impossible to read the writing. This time, Father Salvatore took holy water and sprinkled it on the stain, which disappeared so that he was able to read the letter without difficulty.

An exorcism in the sacristy

One Sunday afternoon in May 1922, some people brought a possessed woman to the sacristy of the little monastery church at San Giovanni Rotondo.

After the evening service of the Benediction of the Blessed Sacrament, Padre Pio went to the sacristy and was confronted with the unfortunate woman. She began yelling, swearing, and blaspheming, while she was shaking with convulsions.

Padre Pio, calm and resolute, began the rite of exorcism. But the woman continued to yell and lash about. The priest went through the rite undisturbed. Suddenly, the demon fled! The woman found her peace and tranquility again, and behaved as if nothing had happened.

Padre Pio pays dearly

In 1964 a young girl was brought from a village near Bergamo to the Capuchin monastery at San Severo. She was possessed, and her friends took her there to see Father Placido de San Marco in Lamis, renowned for his sanctity. They wanted him to free her from the demon. When the girl saw Father Placido, she began to yell curses and blasphemies and even tried to attack him. After some deliberation the friars suggested to Father Placido that he send the possessed girl to Padre Pio at San Giovanni Rotondo.

She reacted in exactly the same way with Padre Pio. At that time Padre Pio did not have the physical strength to deal with such an exorcism, so he only blessed her.

A few days later, other priests, authorized by the archbishop of Manfredonia, tried to exorcise the unfortunate girl and drive out the demon. The fiend laughed at them for trying to exorcise him after they had been eating and drinking instead of praying and fasting! This plunged Padre Pio into great sadness and reflection.

During that night, he was furiously attacked by the devil, who kicked him violently on his spine. He had a bad fall, cutting his eyebrow and causing his face to swell. As he fell, he cried out. His confreres came running and found him in this state. Padre Pio told them he had fallen. He was unable to leave his cell the next morning to celebrate Mass.

Meanwhile, the demon in the possessed girl was yelling that Padre Pio could not come down for Mass because he, the devil, had fixed him up! In fact, the Superior had to announce that Padre Pio would not be coming down that day. The large crowd, gathered at the usual Mass time, was greatly disturbed and disillusioned when they heard this.

That same morning, the Superior of the monastery in San Severo, Father Alberto D'Apolito, arrived at San Giovanni Rotondo where he was told about all that had happened. He asked Padre Pio to confirm what the demon had said. He just said, "It is possible!" Grieved, Father Alberto then told Padre Pio how sorry he was to have sent the possessed girl to him. "You sent me a fine gift, didn't you?" Padre Pio said.

The struggle for this young girl between Padre Pio and the devil, however, was not over. The priest prayed, did penance, and then, barely recovered from his ordeal, went down to celebrate Mass.

This time, when she saw him, the possessed girl shrieked and fainted. The demon left her. She was now calm and at peace. She attended Padre Pio's Mass before going home completely cured. As usual, Padre Pio won this battle with the devil, but he had to pay dearly!

Padre Pio gives Barbablù a kick

In 1946 a woman from Bottegone began to experience persistent physical ailments. She had sudden pains in her knees, her legs, or in other parts of her body, as well as abdominal swelling. This generally happened when she was praying or went to church. The doctors she consulted could offer no remedy.

She spoke of this to a priest from Pistoia who, after giving her a blessing, advised her to see Padre Pio. As soon as she could, she went to San Giovanni Rotondo and took her turn for confession, thinking she could speak to him there about her concerns. As soon as Padre Pio appeared for confessions, her whole body swelled up and she began to yell and scream.

Padre Pio, who recognized the presence of "Barbablù" in the woman, went up to her and kicked her, saying in a commanding voice, "Go! Satan!" The woman fainted and, when she recovered, realized she had been delivered from the devil.

While two policemen escorted her through the crowd, Padre Pio blessed her and said, "Go, thank our Heavenly Mother who has cured you!"

Barbablù takes over Padre Pio's confessional

Father Benedetto from San Marco in Lamis was Padre Pio's Provincial Superior and spiritual director. One day he had to question Padre Pio on his actions, and thus unveiled a nasty trick of "Barbablù." This is what happened.

A young girl from Cerignola had got it into her head that she was damned. She could not find a minute's peace because of this. Her mother decided to take her to Padre Pio so that he could free her from this torture.

They went to San Giovanni Rotondo, and the girl went to Padre Pio for confession. She heard, from behind the grill, what she presumed to be his voice, but it was in fact the demon imitating Padre Pio's voice to perfection! He said to her, "Yes, indeed, you are damned!"

One can imagine the turmoil this girl experienced and the despair she felt! She came out of the confessional more anguished than before and told everyone: "I am damned! Padre Pio himself told me!"

The incident came to the notice of Father Benedetto, who considered it his duty to confront Padre Pio. "Oh! My son!" he said. "What have you done? That poor girl will never find peace again! You must understand that, even if the Lord reveals to you something like this, you are not necessarily authorized to tell the unfortunate person concerned."

Padre Pio was thunderstruck and told Father Benedetto that he would never dream of saying such a thing to anyone. It was clear that "Barbablù" had tortured this girl in order to stir things up and cause trouble. Padre Pio begged Father Benedetto to find the girl and bring her back. She returned and went to Padre Pio for confession, and afterward she was restored to peace.

CHAPTER 10

A Model of a Soldier

When Padre Pio reached conscription age, he was called up for military service just like other young men. This happened in November 1915. His time in the army was short because his state of health did not allow him to fully take part in military life. He was no more than a sampling of a soldier.

This chapter in his career, however, gave him some idea of life in the barracks. He has given us the following delightful accounts of this experience. He said at one point, "I got more out of this ordeal than from any spiritual retreat I have ever made!"

Padre Pio risks a court martial

Padre Pio was called up as Francesco Forgione, serial number 2094/25, on November 6, 1915. He went to the Military District of Benevento and joined the 10th Medical Corps of Naples. He stayed there only until December 10 that year because he had constant attacks of fever. He was discharged for a year. When the year ended, he returned to Naples but stayed only fifteen days. He was again sent home, this time for six months. On his discharge papers, the military authorities had written: "When this leave is over, await further orders."

Months went by, and the military authorities in Naples expected Padre Pio to return. They had obviously forgotten what they had written on his papers. As he did not return, they gave orders to the police in Pietrelcina, his home village, and in San Giovanni Rotondo, his monastery at the time, to find Private Francesco Forgione. This, of course, was Padre Pio's name to the authorities. The police searched everywhere but could not find Francesco Forgione. By chance, they discovered that the soldier and Padre Pio were one and the same person, so Padre Pio, now aware that they were looking for him, went back to Naples.

The military authorities looked on his absence as desertion and punishable by court martial. He showed them his leave papers and told them that the orders he awaited never came through! They accepted his explanation and believed his good intentions, and so he escaped a trial in the military courts.

Private Forgione finds a safe place for his possessions

Contrary to what one would think, Private Forgione enjoyed military service. He was so thin that the uniform hung on him! With his sense of humor, he described himself like this: "My mother made me a man, St. Francis made me a woman (referring to his long, religious habit), and the government has made me a clown!"

When he realized that petty theft was the order of the day in the barracks and that tricks were played on the soldiers by their comrades, Private Forgione tried to find a way of avoiding all this. Finally, he decided he would *wear* everything he owned! He was so thin, and the uniform so big, that he could do this without any difficulty!

One day, he was summoned for a medical examination and asked to undress. Private Forgione calmly began to take off all he was wearing. First came one jacket, then another, a pair of trousers, then a second pair, a shirt and then another, and so on! When the Major saw all the soldier was wearing, he said, "Private Forgione, you are not wearing a set of clothes but a whole store!"

Padre Pio takes a cab in Naples

Shortly after Padre Pio arrived in Naples, he wrote to his father, Orazio, and asked him to send some "goodies" from his village of Pietrelcina.

Uncle Orazio, as he was called, filled a basket with olive oil, goat's cheese, and juicy grapes, and he set off for Naples. The people of his village usually stayed at a boarding house in Naples run by Carolina del Maestro, who was also born in Pietrelcina.

Orazio called a taxi to take him to Carolina's *pensione* or boarding house. The driver pretended to know where he was going, but took his client through all the streets of Naples. When Orazio realized that the man had no idea where he was going, he gave the driver directions, and eventually they arrived at the boarding house. Orazio was annoyed with the driver for giving him the runaround, so, when he paid, he gave the man only fifty cents instead of the seventy-five cents he had demanded. There was nothing the driver could do about it. No one fooled around with Orazio Forgione!

At Carolina's place, he asked about his son. She told him he would be coming soon.

A few minutes later Padre Pio arrived in a cab. Orazio, seeing his son drive up in a cab, asked, "What can be left of the seventy-five cents you got for saying Mass, if you gave fifty cents to the cabdriver and twenty-five cents to the sacristan?" Padre Pio reassured him by saying that he was able to afford this because he was celebrating Mass in a private chapel and was given fifteen lire!

Father and son enjoyed the good food from the village and then went for a walk along the Corso Umberto, also known as Rettifilo (Straight Road). When the time came to part, Orazio was overcome by emotion and began to cry. Padre Pio consoled him by saying he would not be in the army for long.

In fact on November 5, 1917, Padre Pio was sent on leave to Pietrelcina and then to San Giovanni. On March 17, 1918, he was discharged from the army. So ended this brief period of conscription for Private Francesco Forgione!

With a pass and one lira in his pocket

In December 1916 Padre Pio was put on sick leave and set off for Pietrelcina. He had to take the train from Naples to Benevento and then a bus to his village. The train fare was paid by the army, and he was given one lira to cover the rest, that is, his bus ticket and any other expenses.

When he left the military hospital, he walked through Naples enjoying the people of the city with their special way of talking and behaving. On one of the squares he came across a small market that sold everything. Padre Pio thought it would be a nice gesture to bring a little souvenir to his nephews, but how could he manage to do this with one lira in his pocket? A trader came up to him, offering to sell little paper umbrellas. He said they were worth one lira each, but came down to fifty cents, and then forty cents! Padre Pio made some calculations and said to himself, "If I spend my money on these little umbrellas, there will be nothing left!" He left the seller high and dry, and went off to Garibaldi Station.

When his ticket was validated, Padre Pio went to the train and, on the way, met another man selling paper umbrellas. This one called out to him in dialect: "Corporal! Corporal! Buy some of these lovely little umbrellas and give them as souvenirs to your children!" Padre Pio paid no attention, but when the man insisted, he said, "Listen! I don't want them, and I have no need of them. In any case, you are not honest. In the market they sell for fifty cents, and you want 1.50 lire."

The vendor tried again: "Corporal! I have three children. Help me make a little money. Please, please take the umbrellas as souvenirs for your children!"

Padre Pio said, "Will you give them to me for fifty cents?"

The train had started to move, so Padre Pio jumped on and leaned out the window. He was moved with compassion for this poor man and threw fifty cents at him and said, "Here! Take it all and God bless you!"

The man saluted and thanked Padre Pio and, having picked up his fifty cents, went off happily while Padre Pio started on his journey to Benevento.

Padre Pio arrived late at night and tried to find a place where he could spend the long hours before his bus was due to leave—at five in the morning. The waiting room and the bar were full of soldiers, so he went outside and tried walking up and down to keep warm, but he became tired and went back to the waiting room. It was a case of standing room only, but at least he was sheltered from the cold. He spent a few hours like this.

He would have liked to go the bar for some coffee to warm up his insides. How could he do this? Not only were all the tables occupied, but he had only fifty cents in his pocket. Presently he noticed two empty tables and sidled over to one of them, trying not to be noticed. One officer and two non-commissioned officers sat down at the other table. The waiter came and took their order and then moved to Padre Pio's table. There was nothing to do but order a cup of coffee! While waiting, Padre Pio realized that his money was running out and that he might not be able to finish his journey. When the coffee arrived, he drank it very slowly so that he would be able to stay at the table until the bus for Pietrelcina arrived. When it came, Padre Pio went to the counter to pay for his coffee. The waiter told him, "Everything has been arranged! Your coffee is paid for!" How strange!

In the bus Padre Pio went to the back so that he could explain to the conductor, without being noticed too much by the other passengers, that he did not have enough money for his fare, but he would pay it in full upon arriving at the village. The fare cost 1.80 lire! Just before the bus left, a distinguished gentleman got on and sat down beside Padre Pio. The man had a little case and brought out a thermos and a cup, which he filled with hot coffee and gave to Padre Pio, while he drank from the thermos cup. When the conductor came for the tickets, the gentleman said to Private Forgione, "Soldier! Your ticket has been paid for!" Yet again, Padre Pio was taken by surprise and asked, "But who paid for me?" He thought it must have been the gentleman who sat down beside him.

When he arrived at his destination, he looked around to thank his benefactor, but he had suddenly disappeared!

CHAPTER 11

Padre Pio's Sense of Humor

Carlo Campanini, one of Padre Pio's favorite spiritual sons, was a celebrated comedian. He said, one day, "Padre Pio loved to tell jokes, and he was even better at that than I am! He was good at repartee and made quick, funny remarks, like a great actor." And Campanini should know!

L. Bedeschi, a well-known journalist, wrote in *His humor through fifty years as a priest* that Padre Pio was "a great talker, full of life, and brilliant. Up against a wall, he was capable of the most extraordinary rhetoric to extricate himself. As if that were not enough, he could disconcert people by saying something that really sounded bizarre and by making ironic remarks that upset their conclusions. As a good impersonator, he was appreciated even by those who generally could not stand this kind of thing! Above all, his rare sense of humor was evident to everyone."

Needless to say, Padre Pio's humor always had a meaning, and he used it to advantage in his priestly ministry. He told many funny stories, but I present here just a few to give an idea of his kind of humor.

A recruit prepares for the king's visit

A sergeant was preparing a recruit for the king's visit to the barracks. He gave the young man these questions and answers to learn by heart.

Sergeant: How old are you?

Recruit: Twenty-two.

Sergeant: How many years of service have you completed?

Recruit: Two.

Sergeant: Who would you serve most willingly, king or country?

Recruit: One as much as the other, Your Majesty!

The king arrived and, as expected, questioned the recruit. Unfortunately, he did not ask the questions in the same order learned by the recruit. This is what happened:

King: How many years of service have you completed?

Recruit: Twenty-two.

King: How old are you?

Recruit: Two.

The king became impatient and shouted at him: "Who is the bigger idiot here, you or me?"

"One as much as the other, Your Majesty!" the recruit replied.

Padre Pio laughs during a sermon

One of Padre Pio's confreres had seen him laugh during a sermon. Later, when they were together, he asked Padre Pio why he had laughed during a sermon on death. Padre Pio replied in a Neapolitan dialect:

"What could I do about it? I couldn't help it! Some preachers would make you laugh at anything, even when they're talking about death!"

Padre Pio is not afraid of lightning

One of Padre Pio's Brothers was in the corridor with him during a violent thunderstorm. The lightning flashes came nearer and nearer. Terrified, the Brother turned to Padre Pio and said that they could be struck by lightning because they were standing near the electrical power panel. He added, "Father, we should at least move away from the panel. Only yesterday, ten people were killed by lightning!"

Padre Pio replied, "Then we don't need to be afraid. There are only two of us!"

Padre Pio for twenty cents!

Padre Pio told this anecdote one day to some of his friends. The incident occurred in 1922 or 1923 when news got around that he had the stigmata. A photographer, who wanted to take advantage of this situation right away, took some photographs of Padre Pio.

Although the photos were not very good, the photographer had copies made and gave them to a boy to sell for twenty cents each. This boy was selling them a bit too near the monastery when Padre Pio heard him. "You riffraff!" he yelled in a menacing voice, "I'll teach you to sell me for only twenty cents!" The terrified boy ran off.

Padre Pio turned to his friends and said, "They could have sold me for a bit more than that!"

"Go, tell Professor Lunedei . . ."

Carlo Campanini, the comedian, tells of a friend who was under the care of a renowned professor of medicine in Florence. He told the doctor that he was going to San Giovanni Rotondo to see Padre Pio. The professor exclaimed, "What? You are going to see that hysteric? Scientifically speaking, that is what he is. By thinking so much and so often of Jesus Crucified, he created the stigmata in his own body!"

The man did not allow himself to be swayed by these words. He went to Padre Pio for confession, then told him what the doctor had said. Padre Pio replied, "When you see your professor, ask him to think intensely and often of an ox, and see if he grows horns!"

A visit from the President of the Republic

The President of the Republic, Antonio Segni, came one day to visit Padre Pio. In presenting his entourage, the President introduced one of them as Deputy Russo. When Padre Pio heard the word *Russo* (Russian), he asked, "Why have you brought me only one (Russian)? Bring many more to me!"

"With your kind of head, it would be difficult to sin!"

There was a woman, a kind of femme fatale in her younger days, who had become a mere shadow of her former self. The years had taken their toll, and she had become rather ugly.

She reflected on the vanity of human things and felt the need to concentrate on more lasting values. So, she decided to go to Padre Pio for confession.

To get to him she had to register and wait her turn. This woman was not put off by the wait. She wanted to be sure of seeing Padre Pio, so she registered twice! She waited her turn patiently and, when it came, went to confession.

The next day her second turn came up, but, when Padre Pio saw her, he said, "You went to confession yesterday. What else do you want from me?"

"But," the woman said, "since yesterday I might very well have sinned again!"

"Nonsense," he said, "with a head like yours, it would be difficult to sin!"

A humorous meeting

Two comedians went to see Padre Pio one day. When Padre Pio saw them in the corridor, he said, "Just look at those faces!" The man who introduced them said, "Father, these actors have decided to stop working with their legs and start working with their heads."

Padre Pio replied quickly, "They should do that! The important thing is that they get it right!"

When leaving them, he said, "Keep on being a disgrace. When all is said and done, you have never done anything to be proud of. Change that or I will throw you out!"

"Go ahead! This is your chance!"

Father Constantino Capobianco tells of how he was becoming harder of hearing until he could not hear at all. This was very humiliating for him. To help him hear better, the Superior bought him a hearing aid, which helped greatly.

One day in the course of a conversation, Padre Pio asked Father Constantino how much he could hear without the aid. Father Constantino told Padre Pio that he could not hear at all. Padre Pio asked him to turn off his hearing aid for a few moments, then called out to the other friars, "Go ahead, boys! This is your chance to say what you want about Father Constantino!"

"So, who is to blame?"

Father Carmelo da Sessano was Guardian of the monastery when an order came from Rome authorizing a television crew to film a day in the life of Padre Pio. Padre Pio resigned himself to this because the Superior asked him to let the film crew do it, and he thought it would not last very long.

When Padre Pio came down from his cell to say Mass, he was confronted by the film crew who went to work. He then went to the chapel of St. Francis where he celebrated Mass at this time. The noise of the camera disturbed him, and he suddenly turned around and said, "Either you stop or I stop! I will go away and will not say Mass!"

They had to postpone the filming but started again afterward, doing the best they could to catch other features of Padre Pio's day. He cooperated as little as he could and tried to limit the filming as much as possible. When the filming was finished at last, the Superior asked if Padre Pio would see the crew. They wanted to thank him and ask his blessing. He agreed and received the technicians who apologized for having disturbed him. They pointed out to him, however, that it was not their fault, as they had their orders.

Padre Pio said to them good-naturedly, "You had your orders, so it is not your fault. Father Guardian had his orders, so it is not his fault. The Superiors of the Province had their orders, so it is not their fault. The Major Superiors had their orders, so it is not their fault. Well, then, whose fault is it?"

"What do you want for a blessing?
A pail of water over your head?"

Grazia, a young woman of twenty-nine, often frequented the little church in the monastery at San Giovanni Rotondo. She had been blind since birth. Padre Pio asked her one day if she would like to see. Grazia answered that she would like to see if it would not cause her to sin. The priest told her she would be cured of her blindness and sent her to Dr. Durante, an excellent eye surgeon in Bari.

When the doctor examined the blind girl, he realized there was nothing to be done for her. He advised her to go back to Padre Pio and ask for a miracle. But the doctor's wife, who was present, pointed out that if Padre Pio had sent him this patient, it was because he knew something could be done. Why not try? The surgeon was persuaded to do the operation.

He operated first on one eye, and Grazia's sight was restored. Then he did the other, and she was able to see with both eyes. He was astonished and could not find any reasonable explanation! The girl could see.

As soon as she got back to San Giovanni Rotondo, Grazia went to thank Padre Pio. She threw herself at the feet of the priest she was seeing for the first time and told him of her joy, her admiration, and her gratitude. Padre Pio stood still and looked at her, smiling. Grazia then asked for Padre Pio's blessing, and he traced the Sign of the Cross over her. But Grazia continued to cry out, "Bless me, Father! Bless me!" She expected him to take her by the hand as he had done when she was blind. Finally, Padre Pio said to her, "What do you want for a blessing? A pail of water over your head?"

"They sing while I suffer!"

A companion of Padre Pio, who wanted to give him some comfort during the many illnesses he had to endure, told him one day that the people were concerned for his health and were praying for him. Padre Pio said, "That's right! They sing, and I suffer. They are like the rooster that sings while the hen suffers laying an egg."

Conclusion

We are left to wonder at the variety and abundance of Padre Pio's charisms! So many gifts in one person! What is there to say about this? Aside from the unfathomable mystery of God, who calls his creatures to life and involves them in his universal plan by giving them a mission and means to accomplish it, we could also say that there is a "style" that governs the way the divine relates to souls. When someone is given to God totally and completely, God generously endows that person with a staggering variety of gifts that leave us speechless. I am tempted to say that in Padre Pio's case, God enjoyed intervening in the most original and unexpected ways.

Padre Pio, as all his biographers show, had consecrated himself to God from childhood in a total and irrevocable way. And despite all his lengthy struggles against man and the devil, he remained faithful to this gift of himself to God. It is hardly surprising that God showered him with such graces.

There is a lesson here for us. To trust in God and abandon ourselves to him through all the events of life is to attain happiness, if we look at life with the eyes of faith. It is through faith that we come to an understanding of the real meaning of life, as it unfolds here on earth, and in its eternal perspective.

BOOKS & MEDIA

A mission of the Daughters of St. Paul

As apostles of Jesus Christ, evangelizing today's world:

We are CALLED to holiness
by God's living Word and Eucharist.

We COMMUNICATE the Gospel message
through our lives and through all
available forms of media.

We SERVE the Church
by responding to the hopes and needs
of all people with the Word of God,
in the spirit of St. Paul.

For more information visit our website: www.pauline.org.

BOOKS & MEDIA

The Daughters of St. Paul operate book and media centers at the following addresses. Visit, call, or write the one nearest you today, or find us at www.pauline.org

CALIFORNIA
3908 Sepulveda Blvd, Culver City, CA 90230 — 310-397-8676
935 Brewster Avenue, Redwood City, CA 94063 — 650-369-4230
5945 Balboa Avenue, San Diego, CA 92111 — 858-565-9181

FLORIDA
145 S.W. 107th Avenue, Miami, FL 33174 — 305-559-6715

HAWAII
1143 Bishop Street, Honolulu, HI 96813 — 808-521-2731

ILLINOIS
172 North Michigan Avenue, Chicago, IL 60601 — 312-346-4228

LOUISIANA
4403 Veterans Memorial Blvd, Metairie, LA 70006 — 504-887-7631

MASSACHUSETTS
885 Providence Hwy, Dedham, MA 02026 — 781-326-5385

MISSOURI
9804 Watson Road, St. Louis, MO 63126 — 314-965-3512

NEW YORK
64 West 38th Street, New York, NY 10018 — 212-754-1110

SOUTH CAROLINA
243 King Street, Charleston, SC 29401 — 843-577-0175

VIRGINIA
1025 King Street, Alexandria, VA 22314 — 703-549-3806

CANADA
3022 Dufferin Street, Toronto, ON M6B 3T5 — 416-781-9131

¡También somos su fuente para libros,
videos y música en español!